Baseb Inside the Zone

33 Mental Training Workouts for Champions

What if <u>one thing</u> could change EVERYTHING...?

Game. Changer

By Rob Polishook, M.A., C.P.C.

Baseball on the Brain!

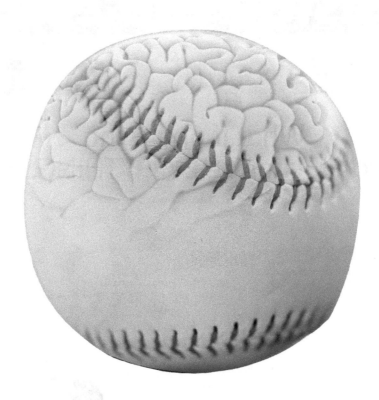

Cover Design by Kellie Patterson

BASEBALL INSIDE THE ZONE
33 Mental Training Workouts for Champions

Published and Distributed by Inside the Zone Sports Performance Group
www.insidethezone.com
rob@insidethezone.com

ISBN 978-0-9891862-4-7

How to Use This Book

Baseball Inside the Zone: Mental Training Workouts for Champions can be read and experienced in different ways. Initially, I suggest browsing through the table of contents to gain a broad overview. You will notice there are four sections, similar to how a game would unfold: Off-the field, Pre-game, In-game, and Post-game. Then browse the individual workouts; each one also has four parts. These include:

- Quotes from the pros

- Principles which serve as a foundation

- A mental training article

- Interactive worksheet which ties the quotes, principles and article together.

These four create what I have coined a "Mental Training Workout." The goal of the workout is to experientially guide you through the mental training concept

I suggest you read the book in one of the following ways:

Start with a random section or specific workout that resonates with you. For example, maybe you're having trouble keeping yourself calm and relaxed before a game? Go to the workout "I'm Nervous! What Do I Do? — Five Ways to Work Through Pre-Game Jitters." After reading the quotes, principles and article, take some time to think about them, and ask yourself a few questions: What does this workout mean to me? How might it apply to my situation? How could I incorporate the principles into my game? If I did, what might happen? Then, pick up your pen and complete the mental training workout. Take your time and approach each workout with P.I.P. (purpose, intention, and passion). Please note: simply reading this book like any other is not going to make a difference in your game, it is key that you think about concepts and put pen to paper expressing your individual experiences. That's when transformation can happen.

Baseball Inside the Zone can also be experienced by simply reading and completing the workouts from the front of the book to the back of the book, highlighting the parts which resonate with you. Or choose a partner and work through the workouts together. This is a great opportunity to share ideas. Additionally, coaches, teachers, parents, and sport psychology professionals can also facilitate the workouts in a group or team setting, encouraging the players to share their experiences. Maybe picking out the key points and how the player could implement the teaching.

Reggie Jackson once said, "you can't steal second base and keep a foot on first base." Remember, every level of baseball will raise a new set of challenges and obstacles. This is not bad; just a fact! Stay patient and stick with it... I promise you... it won't be easy... but it will be worth it!

Contents

How to Use This Book..III

What Are Mental Training Workouts?...1

How Will Mental Training Workouts Help You?... And Other FAQs.................2

Section 1: Off The Field Workouts   5

Workout 1: How Do I Get the Mental Edge? *Unlock the Mystery of the Mental Game*..........9

Workout 2: Winning Within: *More than an Athlete: Person 1st. Every Time* 15

Workout 3: How to Get and Stay Motivated! *Understingng Your Big Why*.......................21

Workout 4: Competeology: *The Key to Winning*..27

Workout 5: So You Want to Win! *What Will It Take?*..33

Workout 6: Goal Setting: *Players Don't Plan to Fail, But They Do Fail to Plan*.................37

Workout 7: What Does it Take to Win? *Awareness and the 5 A's*.............................43

Workout 8: Playing Inside the Zone: *One Pitch at a Time*...................................49

Workout 9: Dream On! *How Imagery Can Help You Win*......................................55

Section 2: Pre-Game Workouts   61

Workout 10: OMG... I'm Nervous! *Five Ways to Work Through Pre-Game Jitters*.............65

Workout 11: How to Play in the Moment: *It's as Easy as Breathing*.........................71

Workout 12: Field Awareness: *Playing With Your Mental Positioning System*................77

Workout 13: Why Can't I Play Games Like Practice? *Five Reasons This Happens*.............83

Workout 14: Concentrate! *Focus on What You Can Control*...................................89

Workout 15: Rituals That Work: *Plan and Prepare for Success*..............................95

Workout 16: Stay Positive! *Seven Questions That Will Improve Your Game*...................101

Section 3: In Game Workouts 105

Workout 17: Between-Pitch Rituals: *Don't Leave Home Without Them!* 109

Workout 18: Tense, Nervous… Can't Relax? *Five Ways to Manage Pressure* 115

Workout 19: Tension, Tears, and Twitches: *The Secret to Managing Stress* 123

**Workout 20: I'm So Tight… *How Can I Loosen Up!?* 123

Workout 21: I SUCK! *How to Tame Negative Self-Talk* 129

Workout 22: You Cannot Be Serious! *Seven Tools to Help You Regain Your Focus* 135

Workout 23: Bottom of the Ninth. Relax! But How? *Five Steps to Closing Out a Game* 141

Workout 24: What Do I Do Between Innings? *Keeping Your Focus in the Dugout* 147

Workout 25: Competing in the Trenchs: *One Part Skill, Three Parts Will* 151

Workout 26: Riding the Waves: *Using Momentum to Win* 157

Workout 27: Get Outta Your Mind: *It's the Only Way to Compete!* 163

Section 4: Post-Game Workouts 169

Workout 28: Losing Stinks! *Dealing With a Tough Loss* 173

Workout 29: Mistakes, Setbacks and Failure: *Dealing With Disappointment* 179

Workout 30: I'm Better! How Could I Lose! *7 Biggest Mistakes the Favorites Makes* 185

Workout 31: Sweet Victory! *Seven Questions to Ask After a Win (or Loss)* 191

Workout 32: Flight, Fight, Freeze: *The Seven Biggest Fears That Paralyze Athletes* 197

Workout 33: I Can't Believe I Choked! *Understanding Slumps, Blocks and the Yips* 203

Conclusion 208

What's Next? 208

Praise for Inside The Zone 209

Biography of the Author 214

About Inside the Zone Sports Performance Group 216

About Rob: The Back Story 217

Acknowledgements 218

Sources 220

What Are Mental Training Workouts?

Baseball Inside the Zone: Mental Training Workouts for Champions allows you, the player, coach or parent, to seamlessly integrate the mental game with adjustments, approaches, strategies, and the physical game of baseball. Dedicating this time and discipline will improve your overall performance on the field. Over the years, I have observed players carve out time for drills and practice, cage work and bullpen sessions, games, and fitness focusing on flexibility, strength, and conditioning. This same commitment and intention must be made for the mental game. It's the "glue" that holds everything together.

Baseball Inside the Zone consists of 33 cutting-edge mental training workouts highlighting specific mental training principle. Specifically, each workout includes quotes from the pros, key principles, an in-depth article, and an experiential interactive workout for the player to complete.

Improving a player's mental game takes time. It's a process, during which the player will undoubtedly experience moments of feeling in control, moments of frustration, and moments where progress simply is not evident. In fact, it is much like a pitcher developing a new pitch. It takes time to develop the proper arm slot and get a feel for the pitch. Then comes the development of commanding the pitch. Followed by building up enough confidence in a game

to implement it. As well as, strategizing in what situations or counts the pitcher feels his new pitch should be utilized. Each step builds on the previous one, like a growing tree: first come the seeds, then the roots, then the trunk, then the branches, then the leaves, and finally the fruits!

The discipline to allocate real time to complete a workout for the mental game demonstrates dedication, understanding, and purpose. Oftentimes, when a player works on the mental game it happens only after they played in a game, drills, fitness, and school work are completed! In many cases, players, parents, or coaches don't even think about the impact of the mental game until a bad loss or slump happens. I know, because this is when most of my clients come to seek my mental training services. In actuality, the loss, or struggle at the plate is not the problem, but a symptom of something else which is behind it.

By reading and completing the workouts in Baseball Inside the Zone players, parents and coaches can follow a fun, systematic, and personally experiential approach to gain confidence in their mental game. Most players don't realize that it is not physical talent that separates players, but how they utilize the mental game. Don't you owe it to yourself as a player to reach your peak performance on the field and start playing *Baseball Inside the Zone*?

How will this book help you?

Baseball Inside the Zone is intended to help you master the mental game of baseball. It is designed to provide you with key mental strategies for specific situations you encounter throughout each game, so that you no longer struggle with distractions, loss of focus, pressure, concentration, making proper adjustments, and prolonged slumps.

Baseball Inside the Zone will help you discover your unique strengths and make them even more potent, while identifying and moving beyond challenges and blocks which get in the way of your peak performance.

Baseball Inside the Zone can help you improve as a player on the mound, in the field, and at the plate without picking up a ball!

It can help you:

- adapt and adjust from pitch to pitch

- play like you do in practice during games

- manage pressure and tension, and slow the game down

- stay focused in the moment, and let go of distracting or uncontrollable factors

- embrace challenges, pressure, and competition

Who should read this book?

Baseball Inside the Zone was written for all athletes of all sports, and especially targeted for baseball players. It will also serve coaches, parents, and even fans to help them understand and relate to what their player is experiencing and feeling. Additionally, it will provide valuable ideas to help them coach and support the individual player. The book provides practical value-added stories, quotes, exercises and worksheets to help baseball players move forward in their journey toward achieving their personal peak performance on the diamond. It will help you be the best version of yourself both on and off the field.

Why is this book different?

Baseball Inside the Zone is an interactive book that is designed to engage the athlete and help them create a personal experience, one which will guide them beyond self-imposed limits, expectations, and mental blocks. *Baseball Inside the Zone* will help the athlete become aware of what makes them unique as a player and how to translate these attributes into their performance on the field.

Baseball Inside the Zone is not written from an ivory tower; in fact, I like to say it's written from getting my uniform dirty right alongside my clients. The chapter ideas all came from my clients!

Baseball Inside the Zone is not written in "psychobabble;" in fact it includes real examples, quotes, and stories from my clients' experiences; as well as observations from watching my clients play. For example, how many of you have said, "I'm better, how could I lose?" or, "I'm nervous, what do I do?"

Most players spend very little time on the mental game. Maybe they read an article here or there, or pick up a quote, but rarely do they apply the information to each pitch throughout a game. This book features stories, workouts, quotes from big leaguers, and articles which highlight specific competitive situations for baseball.

Baseball inside the Zone knows that you are more than an athlete. And your secret to personal peak performance is bringing who you are to what you do. Person first. Every time.

Get ready for a fun ride around the bases. Think of it as your home run trot!

The journey starts now!

Fields of Fear: the Mackey Sasser story
ESPN 30 for 30 short documentary

Mackey simulating a
throw during a session.

Afterwards we headed to
Shea Stadium.

Left to right: David Grand,
Mackey Sasser, Rob
Polishook, Alan Goldberg

Mackey in his element
coaching the Dothan
Governors

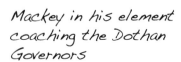

BASEBALL
ZONE
INSIDE THE

Section 1
OFF THE FIELD WORKOUTS

Workout 1: How Do I Get the Mental Edge? *Unlock the Mystery of the Mental Game*..........9

Workout 2: Winning Within: *More than an Athlete: Person 1st. Every Time* 15

Workout 3: How to Get and Stay Motivated! *Understingng Your Big Why*......................21

Workout 4: Competeology: *The Key to Winning*...27

Workout 5: So You Want to Win! *What Will It Take?*...33

Workout 6: Goal Setting: *Players Don't Plan to Fail, But They Do Fail to Plan*......................37

Workout 7: What Does it Take to Win? *Awareness and the 5 A's*..43

Workout 8: Playing Inside the Zone: *One Pitch at a Time*..49

Workout 9: Dream On! *How Imagery Can Help You Win*...55

Off the Field Workouts

To the Child Within

*There's a child inside of you who holds the key to your greatest dreams.
While she may be sometimes frightened by other people and events, she
refuses to let go of those dreams.
She tugs at your leg for attention.
She whines for you to notice her.
She whispers in your ear of all that you can be.
Sometimes you'd just like her to go away with all that silliness.
No such luck. She's too persistent.
She's determined to get noticed.
She refuses to give up.
You've tried to talk some reason into her, but thankfully she won't listen.
Others have told her the "facts" and the limits on what's possible.
She's not interested in their "impossible."
She does not understand "can't."
She doesn't care if others laugh at her dreams, as long as you don't.
She wants you to consider the possibilities.
She wants to show you what she can do.
She will not quit until she's gotten your attention.
Her spirit can't be broken.
She refuses to stay down.
Her resiliency is awe inspiring.
Her enthusiasm is refreshing and boundless.
Harness that child within.
Learn to listen to her.
Let her guide you to your dreams.*

— Dr. Alan Goldberg, author of *Sports Slump Busting*
and co-author of *This is Your Brain on Sports*

Workout 1
Mental Point

Baseball players with the mental edge have the ability to adapt and adjust to overcome adversity, while keeping their focus in the present moment.

How Do I Get the Mental Edge?
Unlock the Mystery of the Mental Game

What the Pros Are Saying

"The mental edge is gained slowly; bit by bit. You grow into greatness."

> — **Rod Carew,** Hall of Fame Infielder, *MLB.com*. Rod Carew's *Hit to Win: Batting Tips and Techniques From A Hall of Fame Hitter*

"I don't know how good I can be. That's what I'm trying to figure out. That's why I do what I do everyday in between starts to prepare myself as best as possible."

> — **Jake Arrieta,** Chicago Cubs Pitcher, Cy Young Award Winner and World Series Champion, *NBCSports.com* (September 5th, 2015)

"I want to get caught up and lost in the process of all things that put you in a position to have a great chance."

> — **Aaron Boone,** New York Yankees Manager, *New York Post* (December 7th, 2017)

Key Principles
1. Focus on process, not outcome.
2. It's not *when* you get there, it's *how* you get there.
3. Success is defined through your values, not from what you do on the field.

How Do I Get the Mental Edge?

Ask any baseball player how important the mental game is—most would say it's between 50% and 99% of competition. Or, as Hall of Fame catcher, Yogi Berra, put it, "Baseball is 90% mental, and the other half is physical." Many ballplayers don't understand how to unlock the mystery of the mental game. Often in pressure packed moments, players' thoughts will get in the way of their ability to perform. Maybe, they are thinking about a previous at bat where they got caught guessing off-speed on an 0-2 pitch, and the pitcher froze them with a fastball inside. In the field, their internal clock is speeding up because they know the runner at the plate is fast, and if a ground ball comes to them, they're going to have to get rid of it quick. They fail to remain grounded in the present moment. Hall of Fame infielder, Rod Carew, stated, "When you learn to believe in yourself, there's no telling how good a player you can be. That's because you have the mental edge." However, the first step begins by asking the right questions.

What is the mental edge? Baseball players who demonstrate the mental edge rise above adversity and adapt to what's happening in the present moment. Other characteristics include patience, calmness under pressure, focusing on what you can control, and letting go of what you cannot. The game of baseball is predicated around failure, so when things go wrong, as they often do throughout the course of a game, the mental edge is necessary to make the proper adjustments and remain in the moment. As a hitter, you may have fouled back a hanging, belt-high curveball because you pulled open on your front side. Rather than focusing on the past, you reset, and on the next pitch you're able to keep your front side locked for a base hit. These players also have the ability to raise their level when it's needed most. Think about 3x Gold Glove and Silver Slugger Award winner, Evan Longoria's 12th inning walk-off home run in 2011, on the last day of the season against the Yankees, which put the Tampa Bay Rays into the postseason!

Who has the mental edge? Two baseball players come to mind. These icons are 13x All-Star, Mariano Rivera and 14x All-Star, Derek Jeter. These two players were on top of the game of baseball for many years. Both have consistently performed at the highest level, and on the greatest stage throughout their careers. In fact, more men have walked on the moon (12) than have crossed home plate against Mariano Rivera in the postseason (11), while Derek Jeter has one of the most impressive October baseball stat lines in the history of the game. In 158 postseason games, he has 200 hits, 20 homers, 18 steals and a .308 average. Both of these players have demonstrated the mental edge through their will to compete, their respect for the game, and their ability to adjust to adversity and pressure-filled situations.

When do you need the mental edge? Performing under adversity is truly the mark of a champion. This is the time the mental edge is imperative. Most ballplayers can win when they are playing well—they have the momentum and their confidence. However, what happens when one day you go 4 for 4 at the plate, and the next day you go 0 for 4 with a couple of strikeouts? It is difficult to remain a consistent hitter if one day you're extremely confident in your swing, and the next day you're thinking your swing is all over the place. Or as a pitcher, what happens when one start, you throw a complete game shutout, and in your next outing you get knocked around? The mental edge is necessary to manage adversity, use setbacks as learning experiences, and be part of your development towards becoming a top player. 6x All-star and 3x Silver Slugger Award winner, Paul Goldschmidt, said, "I took the failure and loss of a strikeout as a learning experience. I was glad I made a mistake because now I'm not going to make it again." Baseball players with the mental edge take little for granted, give a full effort, and trust their process no matter the score or situation.

Where does the mental edge come from?
The mental edge lies within each of us. It starts on the inside and can be cultivated on the outside by people and experiences. The key is to trust the process, do your best, and learn from mistakes, setbacks, and obstacles that occur not just between the white lines, but outside the baseball field as well. The mental edge is built throughout the course of a career. Each stage throughout a ballplayer's life represents insight and knowledge, which shapes his development as a player.

Why is the mental edge important?
Rookie of the Year winner, Aaron Judge, said, "The mental edge is what separates the good players from the great players." It's the glue that holds everything together. When you have it, you exhibit flexibility in situations, accept imperfection, and work with what you have on that given day. Maybe your fastball velocity just isn't there that day, you are having trouble locating, and just don't have your best stuff; however, your curveball is on. Although you traditionally like to pitch off your heater, today you make the adjustment and are working each count and batter around your curveball. The mental edge is the choice to adjust to the situation, stay in the moment, and compete. The mental edge allows you to compete even when you aren't able to bring your best stuff to the ballpark. A great mental approach is the most surefire way to walk into competition with an advantage.

How do I get the mental edge? This is the million-dollar question. We know that having the mental edge is a crucial component of any ballplayer's game. What many of us don't understand is that, similar to confidence and success, the mental edge is a consequence of actions, behaviors, commitment, experience, and discipline, which are all factors that are in your control as a ballplayer! Great players are very aware and trusting of themselves, their instincts, and their personal process. Much like working on your swing in the cage or developing a new pitch, the mental edge takes daily commitment, and requires entering each practice and competition with purpose and intention.

How Do I Get the Mental Edge?

WORKOUT

In your experience, how important is the mental game during each game?

(scale: 1 = not important; 10 = very important) _____

_____

Explain why you gave it this rating:_____

_____

_____

WHAT does it mean to have the mental edge?_____

_____

_____

WHO demonstrates the mental edge? (What player or team?)_____

_____

_____

WHEN is it necessary to have the mental edge?_____

_____

_____

WHERE does the mental edge come from?_____

_____

_____

WHY is the mental edge important?_____

_____

_____

HOW do players get the mental edge?_____

_____

_____

Understanding the above... List three actions you could do right away to improve your mental game by 5%:

1. _____

2. _____

3. _____

What would you have to sacrifice?_____

_____

_____

Is it worth it? _____   **If yes, when will you start?** _____

What specifically would change in your performance?_____

_____

_____

Imagine what it would look and feel like to play with the mental edge... Describe it.

_____

_____

_____

_____

_____

_____

_____

Workout 2
Mental Point

"The foundation is the person.
How you play is a manifestation of
yourself. Your philosophy of self,
determines your philosophy of
your game, including strongest and
weakest points."
— Dr. David Grand

Winning Within:
More than an Athlete: Person 1ˢᵗ. Every Time.

What the Pros Are Saying

"You know baseball is a funny game. You never know where the game will take you. And I've gone though a lot in my life or in my career to be here, and I couldn't be more thankful."
    — **Steve Pearce,** World Series MVP, *ESPN.com*, October 28th, 2018

"We're normal human beings, we have lives outside of baseball. Things can be going wrong in someone's family or anything like that. It's a big part of the game and it could affect you on the field."
    — **Brock Holt,** 2015 All-Star and World Series Champion, Mass Live, May 18th, 2015

"I am a baseball player who lives in his van. I'm a baseball player who loves surfing, photography, traveling, and the outdoors. I'm a baseball player who had cancer. And I love the fact that people know these things about me. I think it's important to tell people who you really are, whether they're your fans or the people you interact with every day."
    — **Daniel Norris,** Detroit Tigers Pitcher, *The Players Tribune*, April 7th, 2016

Key Principles
1. When you bring who you are to what you do, "more" happens.
2. Who you are as a player, and as an individual, are not two separate entities or identities. They are one in the same.

Winning Within

A baseball player is a person first and an athlete second. This idea may seem obvious, especially considering we are born without a glove, bat, and ball in our hands. When we first walked between the white lines to play, we didn't miraculously change identities—we were the same person. When you walk out onto the diamond, you walk out as a whole person with your spirit, story, soul, and everything else that makes you, uniquely you. Yes, this even includes fears and vulnerabilities. All of your experiences allow you to grow, develop, and transform as a person and an athlete. You are more than an athlete: a person first. Every time.

It can be helpful to think of your development as a tree. A tree starts as a seed, and the roots create a foundation, an anchor of sorts. Think of the roots as our values, cultural orientation, work ethic, spirit, stories, and soul. People in our lives, like our parents, coaches, friends, role models, inspirations, and extended family, influence how our roots grow. For example, by encouraging such traits as moral values, personal confidence, self-belief, personal resiliency, and self-empowerment, you will be better suited to face obstacles, setbacks, and life's challenges. Experiences, both positive and negative, that we encounter also influence and cultivate our development.

Consider this statement from Hall of Fame outfielder Ted Williams: "You can fail 7 out of 10 times and still can be a Hall of Fame hitter." Failure is a large portion of this game, but being able to draw from personal experiences, challenges, and setbacks in your personal life, both on and off the field, can make the obstacles that you will face easier to manage and overcome. The stronger the root system, the stronger and more flexible the trunk and branches become.

Often times I share with my clients, "the fruits are a result of the roots." In society, we usually identify with the fruits first. For example, the evolution of Justin Turner did not happen overnight. Justin Turner was a utility player, a career .260 hitter at best. In 2014 he was released and feared that his MLB career could possibly be over. However, Turner decided to recreate himself. He spent countless hours, behind closed doors, reinventing who he was as a ballplayer starting with his mental approach, his body, his swing, and his internal motivation. He is now one of the game's top talents having finished top ten in MVP voting twice since 2014 and being named to the All-Star team in 2017. While the fruits (results) often garner more attention than the roots (process), it's important to remember that the development of an athlete's performance all starts from the roots. Dr. Alan Goldberg, a mental training coach and co-author of *This is Your Brain on Sports*, noted for his work in the field of sports and performance, says, "It all starts with the person—from there, performance happens."

Now, think back to the time you were having a bad practice or bad game. Maybe you were struggling at the plate and had a couple of strikeouts, or as a pitcher, you had trouble with your command. How much of this was because something was just not right in your personal life? Did you have a rough day at school, an argument with a friend, a break-up with boyfriend/girlfriend, or anxiety about what others were thinking? Often times, off-the-field issues and unrelated stressors affect performance on the diamond. Mackey Sasser, Rick Ankiel, Joey Votto, Khalil Greene, and Tiger Woods are testaments to this.

Again, think back…can you remember walking off the field after a heartbreaking loss, dejected and rattled? It could be a game you felt you should have won but you lost your focus and booted a routine groundball. While you know there are 8 other players on the diamond with you, you feel as if you're the only one. Certainly, the next time the ball finds you in the bottom of the 9th with the game on the line, it's likely the image of the previous error you made in that similar situation will flash before your eyes like a shooting star. The mind and body remember!

Lastly, imagine this: As a pitcher, you have an overpowering fastball. In competition, you hear a pop in your elbow and go on the DL for a year. You rehab tirelessly and do everything the trainers have asked of you to get back on the rubber. When people ask how the arm feels, you reply like a warrior holding a shield, "It feels great. Never felt better." However, every time you grip the baseball you're afraid to let it fly because of the fear of the injury returning. As a result, you adjust your mechanics; maybe you change your arm slot, or simply do not throw with the same live-arm action. You go through a period of continually missing locations and get hit harder than ever before. You mentally battle with understanding that you're physically healthy, but you just can't seem to let your arm go with the same live-arm action that you used to display. What's important to understand is that the body "holds" physical and mental trauma. The body will try to protect itself from further injury recurrence. Many ballplayers rehab injuries on a physical level but neglect the mental side.

In ESPN's 30 for 30 documentary called Fields of Fear, former New York Mets catcher, Mackey Sasser, spoke about how childhood experiences, professional injuries, and negative reactions created the perfect storm for his throwing "yips." In the film, he spoke about the work he did with David Grand, Alan Goldberg, and Rob Polishook (that's me!) and how it allowed him to "let go of a 500-pound weight that he was carrying on his shoulders and throw again."

In summary, when a baseball player steps on the field, they are still the same person and carry stress, experiences, and traumas with them. Understanding this dynamic will help them realize it's not about blocking out experiences, fears, and vulnerabilities; rather, it's about learning from them. When a player trusts himself enough to bring who he is to what he does, that's when more happens!

Winning Within

WORKOUT

What's your story? Baseball Journey Line

Chronologically list key moments or experiences in your past that have influenced or shaped the player you currently are. Take into account baseball or non-baseball related key moments, such as meaningful wins or losses, or moments on the field which you learned from, interactions which may have been impactful, challenges, adversity, or obstacles which you overcame, injuries; inspirations, influences, and confidence builders. List these key moments in the order in which they happened.

1. _____
2. _____
3. _____
4. _____
5. _____
6. _____
7. _____
8. _____
9. _____
10. _____

Plan your story...

Plot the 8 key moments from above along the x-axis (start with the oldest events on the left). Then, rate them in terms of impact, i.e. negative or positive, on the y-axis.

Now, connect the dots to get a better picture of the ups and downs of your journey.

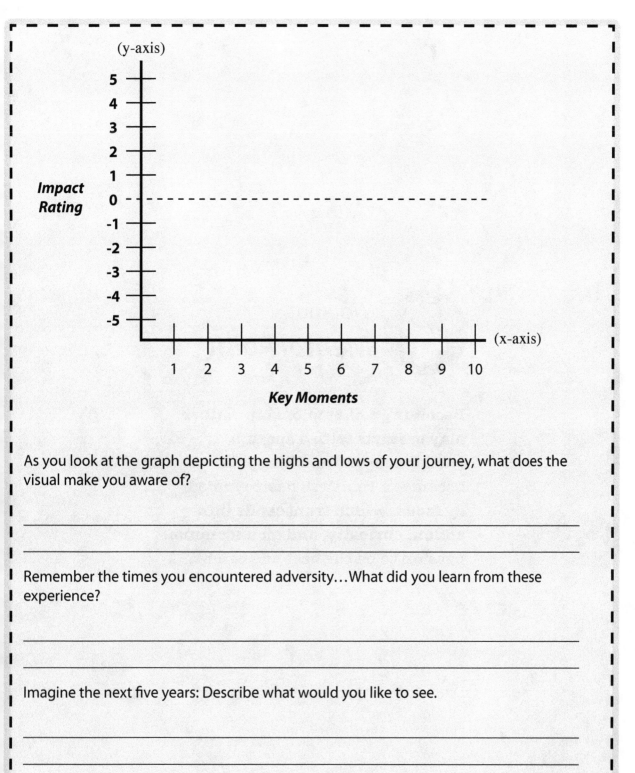

As you look at the graph depicting the highs and lows of your journey, what does the visual make you aware of?

_____

_____

Remember the times you encountered adversity…What did you learn from these experience?

_____

_____

Imagine the next five years: Describe what would you like to see.

_____

_____

_____

Workout 3
Mental Point

**Becoming a championship caliber
player starts with a spark, a
question, a desire. This spark
becomes a limitless desire fueled
by focus, which transcends into
action, curiosity, and an uncommon
passion to be the best one can be.**

How to Get and Stay Motivated!
Understanding Your Big Why

What the Pros Are Saying

"I mean this is a game we get to play. It's the relationships that you make while you play this game- that's what makes this game so special"

    -**David Price**, 7x All-Star and Cy Young Award Winner, *ESPN.com* October 28th, 2018

"I'm playing baseball because I love it, not because I need the money or attention. That is why I've been so dedicated. I've accomplished a lot of things no one ever thought I could, and I've done it from hard work."

    — **Mike Piazza,** Hall of Fame Catcher, *Baseball- Almanac*

"Ever since Will passed away, I've worn a bracelet with his name on it. It helps me remember that connection we had, and the impact Will had on my life…I always felt like I had a secret weapon when I was coming up in the minors. I really tried to visualize Will behind the plate when I was delivering pitches…that's what got me to where I am today."

    — **Carl Edwards Jr.**, World Series Champion, *Players Tribune*, February 21st, 2017

Key Principles
1. Excellence requires uncommon passion.
2. The Big Why is the key to success.

How to Get and Stay Motivated!

Understanding the best way to get motivated and stay motivated is imperative for the success of today's players. Discovering and cultivating this motivation is a crucial component of a player's development, and one of the biggest keys to the mental game. Lasting and passionate motivation begins with the person from the inside out, termed the "Big Why." This "Big Why" is the person's intrinsic, internally driven, reason for wanting to reach his goals.

Identifying and connecting to your "Big Why" may be the most important part in developing your mental game. How many times have you seen a coach help a player work on his craft, while the player shows very little enthusiasm or desire to get better? In this instance, the coach appears to have more energy than the player! Understanding the answer to these basic questions is imperative: Why do you play? What is it about the game of baseball that you love? What are you willing to sacrifice to improve? What are your definitive goals? When a player has a clearly defined "Big Why", he becomes better able to learn from mistakes, bounce back from failure, and push forward to achieve his goals. The "Big Why" ultimately becomes the groundwork for who you are as a baseball player. It is the fuel and the passion that generates unyielding energy to achieve.

Oftentimes, when doing a workshop with a group of young players, I will bring a volunteer to the front and ask him to jump as high as he can from a standing position. Each time I ask him if he can jump higher. After a few jumps, the player usually says, "That's the highest I can go." Urging the player to try once more, only to hear the resignation in his voice, he explains: "I can't go any higher." At this point, I provide some motivation by introducing a reward that is meaningful to him, proposing that if he can jump two inches higher, he will get the reward. Sure enough, in the thousand times I have done this demonstration, the player always strategizes differently, has a higher level of intensity, and 99.9% of the time, the player reaches the higher mark he once thought was impossible.

After experiencing this exercise, the player immediately becomes aware of his increased motivation and sharper focus, which enables him to strive higher. Certainly, offering a prize as motivation is short-lived and at best provides short-term motivation. However, what is important is demonstrating how a player can achieve and accomplish more if they have an intrinsic "Big Why". When the "Big Why" is personal, a player will feel lasting ownership, self-empowerment, and responsibility for his performance on the field.

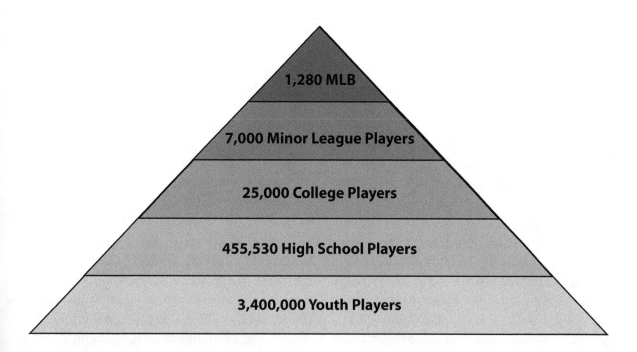

1,280 MLB

7,000 Minor League Players

25,000 College Players

455,530 High School Players

3,400,000 Youth Players

The picture above shows how many ballplayers there are at each level. You can make the argument that the higher you climb up the pyramid, the narrower the difference in talent becomes. Each player has a physical skill set that allows him to compete at an extremely high level. So, what separates a good player from a great player? The answer is the "Big Why". "Why" you play the game! Talent can only take you so far in the sport of baseball, but understanding your why, and what intrinsically motivates you, is what separates a good player from a great player! Understanding your "Big Why" gives you the edge and can distinguish the best from the rest.

Hall of Fame catcher Mike Piazza said, "Nobody wanted me. Scouts told me go to school, to forget baseball. Coaches said. 'You're never going to make it…'"

Nevertheless, Piazza was on a mission, driven by his personal "Big Why". With this motivation, Piazza strengthened his resiliency and ability to adapt and push through the inevitable slumps and struggles that he faced. When failure did arise, Piazza's love of the game and sense of purpose allowed him to dig deeper and maintain his edge over the competition. The "Big Why" helps us understand how the 62nd round pick in the 1988 draft eventually became the all-time home run leader as a catcher.

Once a player understands his goals and his "Big Why" for achieving them, it becomes important to plan measurable and realistic process-driven approaches in order to reach those goals. During this stage, the player must recognize that he has choices and responsibilities in owning his success. Players should understand that they can take two roads. The first road is difficult: it requires sacrifice, hard-work, endless amounts of reps in the cage and on the field, and it even requires failure along the way. However, the reward is a trip on "Cooperstown Drive." The second road is easy. It requires little work, and it's a comfortable path that entails little effort. The destination of this road is called "La-La Land Lane." Think of these two paths as the difference between a player that consistently makes an impact, and a player that never leaves the dugout. Often, I ask players to outline what each road would look like with regard to choices, actions, and behaviors in areas such as family life, schoolwork, and lastly, on the baseball field. The biggest lesson is that players realize that their actions not only on the diamond, but also off the diamond, will directly affect the results. Through this exercise, they can see which road they are following: Cooperstown Drive or La-La Land Lane!

In summary, the "Big Why" is all about motivation, personal empowerment, and the catalyst for transformation. It requires that players make choices and take responsibility for their actions. It is personal because it comes from firsthand experiences, perspectives, and understandings. It simply comes from within! An athlete's "Big Why" will not be sustaining if it only motivates him to be a better athlete. It needs to be big enough to motivate him to be a better person, too! When adversity inevitably arises, or sacrifices must be made, the "Big Why" remains the athlete's most durable source of motivation. Ultimately, the payoff for identifying your "Big Why" is reaching unlimited personal potential, which, in turn, impacts every area of your life!

Inside the Zone
Graffiti Sneakers!

How to Get and Stay Motivated!

WORKOUT

The Big Why is an athlete's key secret to success.

When a player has an internally driven "Big Why" (reason for playing), which is not solely based on winning and losing, they will be more apt to persevere and focus on their process. This "Big Why" will enable them to strive and reach their personal peak potential.

List four reasons you enjoy playing baseball (Big Why).

1. _____
2. _____
3. _____
4. _____

Now, considering the above Big Whys, rank them in order of importance to you:

1. _____
2. _____
3. _____
4. _____

Being aware of your Big Whys, how can they help to motivate you?

_____

_____

_____

_____

By playing baseball, is there a person, player, coach, or team, which you hope to inspire or impact? Explain:

_____

_____

_____

What "character strengths" do you get back from playing baseball?

_____

_____

_____

What's your overall goal as a baseball player?

_____

_____

_____

_____

Bringing my Big Y
to the plate.

Workout 4
Mental Point

The game shouldn't be called baseball. It should be called "adjustments"

> **— Orel Hershiser, Cy Young Award winner and World Series MVP.**

Competeology
The Key to Winning

What the Pros Are Saying

"Enjoying success requires the ability to adapt. Only by being open to change will you have a true opportunity to get the most from your talent."
— **Nolan Ryan**, Hall of Fame Pitcher, *Baseball Almanac*

"How you prepare from the moment you get up is how you start winning the day. It's about becoming very singular in your purpose. It's about dialing that focus down and not letting the outside noise enter. You go to win every pitch, every at-bat, and every play. If you win enough of them, you have a great opportunity of winning a baseball game."
— **Jeff Banister**, Texas Rangers Manager, *Baseballmentalgame.com*, October 11th, 2016

"There may be people who have more talent than you, but there is no excuse for anyone to work harder than you."
— **Derek Jeter**, 14x All-Star and 5x World Series Champion, *Baseball Almanac*

Key Principles
1. Adapting and adjusting are key components of competing.
2. It's not whether you make mistakes, but how quickly you can process and learn from them.
3. Define success based on objectives of improvement, not what the scoreboard says.

Competeology

Did you know that the suffix *-ology* means 'the study of'? For example, *astrology* is the study of stars, *neurology* is the study of the nervous system, and *ideology* is the study of ideas. So, what does this have to do with baseball? I would like to introduce a new '-ology' into the world, one that sets the top players apart from the rest: *competeology*—the study of competing. Understanding how to compete is the key to consistency and long-term success in the sport of baseball.

Success in the sport of baseball is defined by a player's ability to consistently make proper adjustments. Each pitch and swing throughout the game represent new pieces of information. Competeology turns a player into a student, as he learns what the necessary adjustments are to put him in the best position to be successful.

By successfully utilizing the eight tenets of competing that are discussed below, you can earn your Ph.D. in competeology. More importantly, this applied degree will position you to become the best version of yourself both on and off the field.

1. Cultivate a growth-based attitude vs. a fixed attitude: Carol Dweck, in her book *Mindset*, says that a competitor would always display a growth attitude. He understands that his development is a process, and while a strikeout or a short outing on the mound may hurt, there are lessons that can be learned. Competitive players view mistakes and failures as an opportunity to grow and develop. They understand and process what caused their mistake, and mentally make the proper adjustments to prepare themselves for their next opportunity. Suppose a hitter gets around a middle away pitch and rolls over on it for a soft groundball out. A ballplayer with a fixed mentality sees their talent as unchangeable and gets exceedingly frustrated with setbacks; their mistake becomes their center focal point, and they begin to tailspin. However, a competitive ballplayer feels what they did wrong and makes the proper adjustments, setting the state for future success and positive development.

2. Focus on what you can control and let go of the rest: A competitive ballplayer stays focused on what he can control: things such as effort, energy, and bouncing back from adversity—to name a few. A pitcher may throw a perfect pitch, but the hitter manages to poke it to the outfield for a base hit. The result is something that is out of your control. How you react, adjust, and follow through with the process of the next pitch is something that is in your hands! You must understand that you cannot control how well your opponent plays, the field conditions, or winning and losing. When a competitor focuses on his own game, executing his game plan, and making proper adjustments each pitch, he always walks away knowing he did his best on that day.

3. Adapt and adjust to situations: A competitor is constantly adjusting and adapting in-between each pitch. In baseball, even the slightest adjustments can make a difference. What's most important is to acknowledge what is happening and bring your attention to aspects of your game that you can control. Too often in pressure moments throughout a game, players get caught up solely on the result. Focusing on the result creates anxiety and tension, because the hitter's main focus is on something that is out of his control, which is the result of his at bat! This singular focus takes them away from a key question: What can I do *now, in this moment,* that I can control, that puts myself in the best position to be successful?

4. Learn from mistakes: Babe Ruth was noted for saying, "Every strike brings me one step closer to my next home run." Babe understood that mistakes, setbacks, and failures happen. In baseball, failure should be expected, encouraged, and most importantly, used as a stepping-stone towards your growth and development as a ballplayer. Mickey Mantle once said, "During my 18 years, I came to bat almost 10,00 times. I struck out about 1,700 times and walked maybe 1,800 times. You figure a ballplayer will average about 500 at-bats a season. That means I played 7 years without ever hitting a ball." Mistakes and failure, in the game of baseball, become setbacks only if the player does not learn from them. Mistakes may hurt but are a necessary part of being an all-star.

5. Never, ever, ever give up: Competing means never giving up. A true competitor understands the baseball season is a marathon, not a sprint, and there are going to be days where a hitter's timing just isn't there, and a pitcher just doesn't have his best stuff. A competitive player accepts adversity and views those days as a challenge. A competitive baseball player doesn't mind winning a tight ball game in extra innings or playing from behind. They have perspective, and they understand that every situation throughout the game is a learning experience, and what happens next is the most important thing.

6. Get comfortable being uncomfortable: Former MLB outfielder and Manager Lou Pinella said, "You have to learn how to get comfortable being uncomfortable." A competitive baseball player understands there are moments throughout a game where they may have to take a calculated risk, or step outside the comfort of their game plan in order to be successful. As a result of these adjustments, the competitive player will push himself, and be more in-tune with what's happening now. He understands that by embracing the idea of getting comfortable being uncomfortable, his game will become stronger and reach another level.

7. Be aware and make high-percentage choices: In baseball, we often draw a parallel of making high-percentage choices to discipline. For example, a disciplined hitter consistently lays off pitches out of the zone. The competitive player makes the smart play, based on the situation in the game. An outfielder plays a hard-sinking line drive on a hop because the bases are loaded, it's late in the game, and his team is up three. He could dive, and make a spectacular catch, but he would be risking potentially missing it, and letting all the runners score and tie up the game. The competitive player is always conscious of how to approach different situations throughout the game.

8. Sportsmanship: A competitor respects himself, his opponent, and the game. His focus is on playing hard for the entire game. This allows him to play free, and adapt and adjust to different situations, either on the mound, in the field, or at the plate. Competitors don't hold on to the expectations of others—rather, they acknowledge their opponent's tendencies as a way to gain a competitive edge and stay a step ahead. This mindset allows them to focus on what they can control and adjust in their own game to perform at a consistently high level for a full 9 innings. A true competitor brings a mindset to the field that recognizes that their opponent is not the enemy, but rather views them as a challenge, an opportunity, and a partner that is necessary to bring their play in-between the white lines to the next level.

By following the above tenets of Competeology, you will put yourself in the best position to succeed on the field. These concepts are all within a player or team's control and will therefore increase confidence throughout each game. They will help you to stay present in the moment, instead of worrying about results, focusing on the past, or looking ahead to the future. Lastly, they will help you manage adversity in a game. Ultimately, following the tenets of Competeology will free you to learn and develop every time you step onto the field.

This is a key to sports success!

Competeology

WORKOUT

com·pete (kəm·pēt′): 1. from late Latin competere: to strive together, meet, come together, agree; from com- [together] + petere [to seek]; 2. to enter into or be in rivalry; contend; vie (in a contest, athletic meet, etc.).

Name two players who, in your opinion, compete well.

Player #1: _____   Player #2: _____

List the characteristics, attributes, or behaviors that make them good competitors.

Player #1:   **Player #2:**

_____   _____

_____   _____

_____   _____

_____   _____

_____   _____

Is there anything on this list that the player cannot control?_____

Recognizing this, what does this mean for you?_____

Identify the top three characteristics, attributes, or behaviors from above that, if you improved, you would see the biggest results:

1. _____

2. _____

3. _____

What would happen or be different if you improved on the above things?

_____

_____

_____

Workout 5
Mental Point

A player needs to make a choice: That is, to trust their training, themselves, and their individual process. These choices pertain to what a player can control and what they cannot.

So You Want to Win!
What Will It Take?

What the Pros Are Saying

"Sometimes your drive to be the best is going to push you right up to the edge of complete disaster… just take a deep breath, and slow down."
> — **Chipper Jones,** Hall of Fame 3rd Baseman, *The Players Tribune*, June 12th, 2017

"Every day is a new opportunity. You can build on yesterday's success or put its failures behind and start over again. That's the way life is, with a new game every day, and that's the way baseball is."
> — **Bob Feller,** Hall of Fame Pitcher, *Chicken Soup for the Baseball Fans Soul: Inspirational Stories of Baseball*, by Jack Canfield, October 10th 2001, Page 229.

Key Principles
1. When you let go of expectations, you let go of what's out of your control.
2. The more emphasis that is placed on the outcome of the game, the less time there is to concentrate on what's happening in the game.
3. A key question to ask yourself: How can I put myself in the best situation to be successful?

So You Want to Win!

Jackie Robinson said, "Baseball is like a poker game— nobody wants to quit when he's losing; and nobody wants to quit when you're ahead." All ballplayers have one common trait, they all want to win! However, what separates a good player from a great player is the ability to focus on what they can control and let go of what they cannot control. When a player's focus is consumed with the desire to only win, they miss the opportunity to focus on what they need to do each pitch to be successful. Baseball is unique, each pitch presents a situation that is new and different from the previous pitch. If our mind is focused exclusively on the outcome, there is little opportunity to prepare yourself mentally for what needs to happen in that specific moment, during that specific pitch.

Baseball players can put themselves in the best situation to be successful when they remember that winning is a by-product of letting their training and instincts take over. Therefore, their attention should be harnessed around being in the present moment each pitch, and not drifting on uncontrollable factors such as, previous performances, or future outcomes.

Being present each pitch, allows you to make adjustments. When you adapt and adjust, the game will take care of itself. Certainly, the game of baseball is heavily based upon educated guesses, statistical probabilities, and understanding tendencies. However, players must also embrace the aspects of the game, which are simply unknown. When this happens 3 things can happen:

- **The athlete finds they are not good enough on that day to win.**

- **The athlete learns what skills need to be honed for the next event.**

- **The athlete exceeds their wildest expectations...**

How high can YOU fly?

So You Want to Win!

WORKOUT

Derek Jeter said, "If you're going to play at all, you're out to win." Every player's ultimate goal is to win!

However, what do you do to separate yourself from other players on the diamond? The will to win is not enough. Most players don't realize that winning is the consequence of taking specific actions. Preparation creates separation!

Being able to identify what specific actions are necessary to effectively improve your game puts each player in the best possible position to become their best.

On each line below, list the actions that are necessary to prepare yourself to be in the best position to compete, and give yourself the best opportunity to consistently play at your highest level.

Win

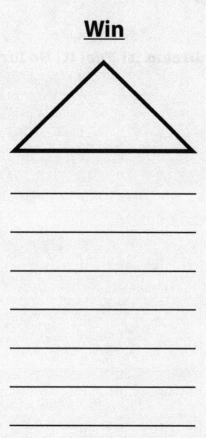

_____

_____

_____

_____

_____

_____

Workout 6
Mental Point

See it! Dream it! Feel it! Go for it!

Goal Setting:
Players Don't Plan to Fail, But They Do Fail to Plan

What the Pros Are Saying

"If you don't set goals, you'll never reach them. Take any player in the major leagues: I'd say just about every one of them had a dream— a goal— to be a big-leaguer when they were kids. It wasn't an easy goal, but it was a reachable one, and that's important."

— **Yogi Berra,** Hall of Fame Catcher, *What Time Is It? You Mean Now?* By Yogi Berra, 2003

"It's such a result driven game, but the process is what is important. You have to have things you can rely on when you look in the mirror at night."

— **Jay Bruce,** 4x All-Star, *Bleacher Report*, May 11th 2015

"If they're not laughing at your dreams, you're not dreaming big enough."

— **Bryce Harper,** 6x All-Star and MVP, Washington Nationals Outfielder, *"Talk Nats" Website*, November 20th 2015

Key Principles

1. Goals act as a compass, guiding you in a direction towards success.
2. Define success based on your individual improvement, not the outcome.
3. Focus on the process, what you can control, and your development.

Goal Setting

Goal setting is a crucial part of the mental game in baseball. Three-time World Series champion pitcher, Jon Lester, said this about goals: "You can work as hard as you want, but if you don't have the right attitude, it's not going to get you anywhere. The goals you set have to be high, to the point where you almost can't reach them. If you set the same goals that you consistently reach every year, you're not making yourself better."

If you were driving from New York to California, would you do it without a GPS or map? The answer is no! Without proper directions, you would get lost and never reach your destination. Like a map, a baseball player uses goals to keep driving forward and to continually improve. If you want to be your best, setting goals and creating an approach to reach them is the best way. Goals helps you stay committed and focused.

Goals should be challenging, individualized, and intrinsically motivated. Goals must be message-specific, so the player knows what he is trying to accomplish. As well as, time-specific, which will hold the player accountable. Goals should be written down and put in a place where a player can see them every day.

There are two types of goals. The first is an outcome goal. This goal focuses on the end result. The second is a process goal, which focuses on the steps that a player can take in order to reach the result. While an outcome goal may be to win the game, the process goal would ask, "What do I need to do to win? What steps must I take? And, how and when must I take them?" Outcome goals are out of a player's control, while process goals focus on aspects of the game that the player can control. For example, a pitcher cannot control the results of his outing. However, he can control how much he prepared, how he warmed up, and how he approached each batter. Process-driven goals can include time in the gym, running extra after a start to increase a pitcher's endurance, or a shortstop taking extra feeds from a second baseman to work on his transfer and footwork. All-Star Raul Ibanez said, "At the end of the day you have your long-term goals, but I'd define success through my daily goals. They help me with my consistency and routine. If I could come in every day and do the mundane and the everyday normal stuff with the same zest and passion, I knew I would have a much greater opportunity to be successful." Similarly, when a baseball player focuses on process-driven goals, and setting a standard to get better every day, the result will usually take care of itself.

An important aspect of goal setting is determining where the player currently is in regards to reaching the goal. A realistic and objective view will help the player become more aware of his situation and understand what he has to do to achieve his goals. Many players only focus on results-oriented goals, and there is a big downside to this approach. Blue Jays Scout, Steve Springer, said, "You can do everything right and go 0-for-4. How can that be? You can hit three rockets right at somebody…. but your batting average goes down." An outcome or results-orientated player would focus only on the fact that the box score read 0-for-4, rather than focus on the fact that he got the barrel on 3 balls, and his bat path through the zone is consistent. As he heads into the next game, he can feel positive about his approach, and know that little extra is necessary and continue swinging the way he has, and the ball will start to fall.

Both outcome and process-driven goals are important. I recommend that a player establish his outcome goals, and then determine the process goals to reach them. 2x Silver Slugger Award winner, Jay Bruce, is a perfect example of someone who decided not to get caught up in outcome goals:

"The approach I've started to take over the past year is quantifying success in a different way. I ran into the problem where no matter what I did, I was wondering why I wasn't doing more. Getting in good counts, not getting overanxious, those are things I can control. That's how I quantify success now. So, you're not chasing the 2-for-4s or 3-for-4s. You're chasing good pitches to hit and mental preparation and the work you do in the cage."

As Dr. Alan Goldberg, noted mental training coach, says, "Once the competition starts, the outcome goal should be parked at the gate and the athlete should only focus on the moment and the process of what they need to accomplish." Interestingly, research has confirmed that reaching process goals not only enhances performance, but also reduces anxiety and builds a sense of confidence.

See the goal, feel the goal, reach the goal!

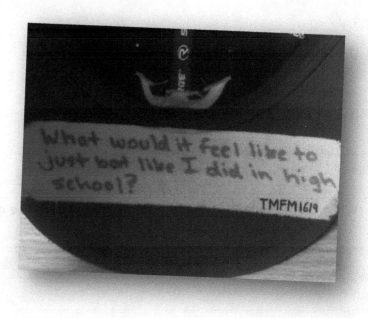

Goal Setting

WORKOUT

What is a goal you want to accomplish?

_____

_____

Why is this goal meaningful to you?

_____

_____

Rate, on a scale of 1-10, where you are now towards achieving this goal (10 = achieved goal).

_____

What are three steps that you must do to achieve this goal?

1. _____

2. _____

3. _____

Do you have the skills to do these?

_____

If not, what skills are necessary to develop?

_____

_____

What can you do immediately to help you reach the goal?

_____

_____

_____

What can you do in the long term to reach this goal?

_____

_____

_____

In attempting to reach this goal, how hard do you think it will be?

_____

What could stop you?

_____

_____

Will you let it?_____

_____   _____
Signature   Date

Workout 7
Mental Point

Awareness and the 5 A's is a formula for problem-solving on the field. It is an essential component of becoming a good competitor and a well-rounded ballplayer.

What Does it Take to Win?
Awareness and the 5 A's

What the Pros Are Saying

"I work every single day. I know what I am capable of doing. Just trust the process and go out there and mimic, mimic, mimic to get a really good and consistent feeling. I try not to focus on the outcome of the at-bats, but the feelings of them."
> — **Andrew McCuthchen,** 5x All-Star and MVP, *MLB on CBS,* 2014

"That is why I love baseball so much – because you measure yourself every night. You have to. Don't focus on the result. You focus on the process. You focus on what you can control, what I did well, what I didn't do well, reevaluate, and then come back."
> — **Raul Ibanez,** 2009 All-Star, *Brian Cain's Peak Performance Podcast.* (N.d)

Key Principles

1. Change starts with Awareness, Acknowledgment, Accountability, Adaptability, Adjustment, and Assessment. Only through knowing where you are, can you get to where you want to be.
2. Setbacks provide a place for a fresh start.

What Does it Take to Win?

Who do you consider a hero? How about Captain Sullenberger? He was the U.S. Airways captain who safely landed Flight 1549 on the Hudson River and saved the lives of 155 passengers on January 15, 2009. Now think about baseball legends, and Hall of Famers, such as Kirby Puckett or Ken Griffey Jr. These heroes and legends have common characteristics: courage, fearlessness, and calm under pressure, to name a few. In order to be a hero or one of the game's all-time greats, you must be able to manage adversity, embrace challenges, and display the ability to adjust to each moment and situation. Hall of Fame pitcher, Nolan Ryan, said, "One of the beautiful things about baseball is that every once in a while, you come into a situation where you want to, and where you have to, reach down and prove something." Embracing adversity in pressure packed situations is not only an opportunity to shine, but also a chance to dig deep and realize what's necessary to be the player you want to be.

We often get mesmerized by the winners, lauding them as super heroes. Yet, the most important component is "what it took" to make victory possible. How do they compete so hard, so effectively, and so consistently? Baseball's champions became that way by overcoming adversity, embracing challenge, and making the appropriate adjustments continually when the game is being played on the greatest stage. There is a saying, "You can't change the wind, but you can change the direction of the sails."

We have all seen players continually do the same thing leading to the same results. Think about a pitcher who has no awareness that the hitter he is facing likes the ball on the inner half. He keeps trying to go in on him, until the batter turns on one and sends it into the stands. How about the hitter who his continually drifting out over his front foot and producing soft ground outs, and refuses to make the adjustment to hit against his front leg, to help him drive the ball, and keep his weight centered? Lastly, consider a pitcher who doesn't adjust to the umpire's strike zone and continually throws balls. Einstein said, "The definition of insanity is doing the same thing and expecting different results."

Probably the most important component of baseball, and life, is the ability to be conscious of a situation and adjust to it. Baseball requires an adjustment on each pitch. Therefore, baseball players need to be great problem-solvers. In order to do this, it's imperative to have a framework in place that you are able to systematically apply. The remainder of this workout will focus on this framework, and what I believe to be the most essential mental characteristics for improvement, success, and ultimately reaching your personal peak performance as a ballplayer. This framework includes awareness and the five A's: acknowledgment, accountability, adjustability, adaptability, and assessment. Without this framework, a baseball player will be unaware of the present moment, and consequently unable to make the proper adjustments.

Awareness: The first step in solving any problem is having awareness—without being aware, a player is unable to assess and determine the current reality of a situation. Awareness entails simply and non-judgmentally observing what is happening. In different situations, this is especially critical, as momentum and circumstances can shift dramatically on one pitch. Remaining in the present allows you to accurately assess a situation and adjust and position yourself accordingly. If you are stuck on the previous pitch, or on a situation a few innings prior, your perception of the situation on that very pitch will be skewed—and similarly, if you are focused on the future, you will be unable to accurately see what is unfolding in front of you.

Acknowledgment: By acknowledging a situation, you do not necessarily have to like it. If your team is losing by 2 runs late in the game, and you're down 1-2 in the count, by acknowledging what this is happening, you can then decide what you can do about it, and how to approach the situation to put yourself in a position to be successful. Baseball players often say, "Why should I acknowledge it? That implies complacency." This is not so. Acknowledgment simply means that you're aware of the current reality of the situation. In effect, I'm suggesting that this provides a choice and the opportunity to either make a change or do nothing. For example, for a hitter that is 0-for-3, and down 1-2 in the count, he could choose

to make the adjustment to keep his swing short and fight off pitches until he got one he could drive. Even though his team is losing and he's having a tough day so far at the plate, maybe this is an at-bat where he gets on base and start a rally for his team. Remember, in baseball, it only takes one pitch!

Accountability: If a player does not take accountability, he will blame the circumstances on someone, or something, else and nothing will change. This attribute can be painful but refer to this saying: "It may hurt, but the truth will set you free." For example, All-Star catcher, Yonder Alonso, took accountability for his poor offensive performance in 2016. He admitted that he was less than thrilled with many of his at-bats and felt that far too many of them were soft outs. He took accountability for constantly chasing bad pitches out of the zone. As a player, the first step in improving your game is to look at your own personal role in the defeat or failure and take a real inventory of what you must do to improve. For Yonder Alonso, that meant taking full accountability for his approach, and making the adjustment to focus on things he could control. He stated, "One of the things you can control is the pitch you swing at, so trust your swing and swing at pitches you can handle."

Adaptability: This refers to adapting internally and responding to the situation during the game that puts you in a position to be able to perform at your best—in other words, being able to mentally reframe a situation. Once a player can go from the negative to the neutral (or, preferably, the positive), they can change the situation towards their advantage. Internal adaptation is imperative—without this, the actions will have no power, passion, or meaning. Often, a player needs to just change his mindset, and emotional status, rather than his strategy, to earn success. For example, 2x All-Star and Rookie of the Year Award winning closer, Huston Street, said this about closing games out under pressure situations, "What is pressure? When you break it down, it's nothing more than an emotion. Emotions are a product of the brain, and therefore if you control the brain, you control its reaction to these situations. In other words, pressure is a choice. You choose to think about 35,000 people screaming or the tying run on second, or you choose to think about what pitch you want to throw, where you want to throw it, and why you want to throw the pitch."

Adjustability: This refers to making changes in physical or technical strategy, based on the situation. In Game 1 of the 2017 World Series, George Springer went 0-for-4 with 4 strikeouts. Going into game 2, he was 3 for his last 30. Clearly, his swing and approach at the plate were not in sync, and pitchers were exposing him. Springer said, "I just think when the lights turn on even brighter you tend to subconsciously press, and you want to succeed so bad that you start to do things that you wouldn't do, or you start to come out of an approach that has worked the whole year." Springer made the physical adjustment at the plate to simplify his swing, and to simply set the tone as a leadoff hitter like he had done all season. The Houston Astros went on to win their first World Series in franchise history, and George Springer was named MVP.

Assessment: This is continual and must be done after a player has made adjustments and adapted. Oftentimes, a player is very close to achieving a goal. However, just one or two more tweaks are needed. Think about as a hitter, or pitcher, how many times you have made an adjustment or tweak after just missing a ball and fouling it straight back or choking your curveball a little too much and not getting the break you want on it. The adjustment step allows you to tweak the facet or area of the game you need to. Without the assessment, it is not possible to determine the results of the previous steps. Additionally, this step allows the entire process to begin again, en route to achieving your goal.

Awareness and the 5 A's is a formula to problem solving on the field and in life. This formula is used by great leaders in the game like Joe Torre or Tony La Russa, and some of the most clutch players, like World Series MVP Madison Bumgarner, and NLCS MVP Daniel Murphy. Think about what it takes to accomplish anything significant in life. Inevitably, awareness and the 5 A's will be necessary, whether it be taking a test, or winning a game. Remember, you can't be your best unless you overcome adversity. The only way is to be aware of it, acknowledge it, be accountable, internally adapt to it, externally make the required adjustments, and then assess what needs to be done and get ready to start progressing, and developing into the player you were meant to be! Are you ready? Start now!

What Does it Take to Win?

WORKOUT

The solution to any problem starts with awareness!

Awareness: Name a specific baseball situation that is troubling you. (describe it)

_____

Acknowledgment: What can you do to acknowledge the situation?

_____

Accountability: What can you do to take accountability for the situation?

_____

Adjustability: What can you do to physically adjust to change the situation?

_____

Adaptability: What can you do to mentally adapt to change the situation?

_____

Assessment: Based on the previous steps, how would you assess things?

_____

Workout 8
Mental Point

**The gift of the body is that it is
always centered and present.**

Playing Inside the Zone:
One Pitch at a Time

What the Pros Are Saying

"When I am in the zone, I feel prepared and I just go moment to moment-from one doing to another. It is simple. No thinking is involved. I don't think ahead. All of a sudden I find myself on second base and the runners have been driven in."

> — **Craig Biggio,** Hall of Fame Utility Player, *Psychology of Champions: How to win at sports and life with the focus edge of super athletes,* by James J. Barrell and David Ryback

"In the zone, everything is in slow motion. I can slow the ball down and almost stop it. Doesn't matter who is pitching… I can hear the ball and see the seams. I know what the pitcher is going to throw. I am relaxed and focused on a good smooth swing. I am very quiet 'inside.'"

> — **Ken Griffey Jr,** Hall of Fame Outfielder, *Psychology of Champions: How to win at sports and life with the fo-cus edge of super athletes,* by James J. Barrell and David Ryback

Key Principles
1. Try softer, not harder.
2. Trust yourself—the real answers are inside.
3. Remember your training—trust your instincts.

Playing Inside the Zone

The 'zone' is a state of being entirely in the present, free of all distractions. A state of being that exists within each of us. Playing inside the zone requires a player to be aware, yet not *over-think*, *judge*, or *over-try*. This state requires an implicit acceptance of what the athlete is experiencing at that particular time. It is a state where the athlete no longer analyzes technique but, rather, just plays, flows, and competes. Paradoxically, when an athlete plays inside the zone, the result is usually well beyond expectations. The result: a smooth, harmonious, effortless flow of energy that produces a limitless performance.

These moments are also called 'peak experiences' by the humanistic psychologist Dr. Abraham Maslow, whose research shows that those who achieve these types of occurrences feel 'more integrated;' 'at one with the experience;' 'relatively egoless;' 'at the peak of his powers;' 'fully functioning;' 'in the groove;' 'free of blocks, inhibitions, cautions, fears, doubts, controls, reservations, self-criticism;' 'spontaneous and more creative;' 'in the here and now;' 'non-striving, non-needing, non-wishing... he just is.' To sum it all up: The feat being attempted is effortless, like flowing water.

As athletes, we are all capable of playing inside the zone. It is a natural state that is experienced, not invented. It is not a destination that you travel to; rather, it is a place that, when you let go of all the distractions within and stay present, will find you. This feeling is aptly addressed in the 2000 movie "The Legend of Bagger Vance," starring Will Smith as the caddy, Bagger Vance, and Matt Damon as the famous golfer, Rannulph Junuh. Vance says to Junuh: "Inside each and every one of us is one true authentic swing... Somethin' we was born with... Somethin' that's ours and ours alone... Somethin' that can't be taught to ya or learned... Somethin' that's got to be remembered... Over time the world can rob us of that swing... It can get buried inside us under all our *wouldas* and *couldas* and *shouldas*... Some folk even forget what their swing was like... Close your eyes... feel the ball..."

Playing inside the zone is the birthright of every person; in fact, each of us has already experienced this seemingly unattainable state as a young child. Born into this world, the unassuming child breathes deeply and instinctively through his or her nose, just like the cheetah, the world's fastest land animal. We learn best when we're young, free from stress and outside distractions that pull us away from the present moment.

Taking your first steps as a child requires trust in self, determination, and trial-and-error. Most children learn to walk before their parents actually teach them. They learn through observation, natural instinct, and modeling others around them. Through this process, children learn to walk— gaining confidence in the natural, instinctual learning process that operates within them. Conversely, parents watch their children's efforts with love and interest, but usually without much interference. When a child loses his or her balance and falls, the mother doesn't condemn the child as clumsy or uncoordinated; she doesn't even feel bad about the tumble. She simply notices the event and provides a kind word, support, and usually a loving gesture of encouragement. Consequently, a child's progress in learning to walk is never hindered by the idea that he or she is not doing better. If we could only treat our teenage and adult athletic endeavors—tennis, baseball, football, gymnastics, swimming, etc.—as we do a child learning to walk, we would make tremendous progress toward uninhibited improvement, playing in the zone, and achieving effortless peak performance.

Michelangelo, the infamous Italian sculptor and creator of the *David*, provides a classic metaphor of focusing on the process and playing inside the zone. He sculpted the Renaissance masterpiece from 1501 to 1504. Undeterred by the challenging task of carving a statue out of a mere slab of marble, Michelangelo had a vision of the finished product; he worked under the premise that the image of *David* was already in the block of stone, a concept referred to as *disegno*. He chipped away at the stone and brought out what others could not even imagine. He saw and knew what others didn't. The marble he was chipping away was a metaphor for the distractions, limitations, fears, anxieties, negative self-talk, and uncontrollable events that get in most people's way. Michelangelo knew *David* existed, but he had to let him appear. Similarly, our best performances are waiting to happen once we let go of distractions, fear of failure, and our ego.

It can be difficult to play in the present. However, by focusing on your breath, present situation, and the process, the zone can be uncovered. While the past can be helpful to learn from, and the future represents goals to be achieved, it is imperative that when performing, an athlete lets go of distractions and just competes in the present moment.

The gift of the body and our senses is that it is always centered and present. To move into the part of you that has the power to transform your life experiences and perform without limits, you must bring your awareness to your body, your breath, your senses, and start from the inside out, much like the eye of a hurricane: still on the inside and unpredictable on the outside. Bagger Vance knew this. He said, "There's only *one* shot that's in perfect harmony with the field... One shot that's his authentic shot... there's a perfect shot out there tryin' to find each and every one of us... All we got to do is get ourselves out of its way, to let it choose us... Seek it with your hands. Don't think about it... Feel it."

Playing Inside the Zone

WORKOUT

Remember a time... when everything was flowing and you were playing Inside the Zone:

When was it?

_____

What time was it?

_____

Where was it?

_____

How old were you?

_____

What were you wearing?

_____

What was the weather?

_____

Who was watching?

_____

_____

What did it feel like?

_____

_____

_____

What smells did you notice?

_____

What was happening?

_____

_____

_____

What sounds did you notice?

_____

What was your sense of time?

_____

What was going through your head?

_____

_____

Overall, what words or images come to mind?

_____

_____

What else do you remember about that time you were playing Inside the Zone?

_____

_____

_____

Connecting to your 'Inside the Zone' image is similar to how the pros use their routine in the on-deck circle, and before each pitch when they're inside the batter's box or focusing on their breathing while taking signs from the catcher. They perform a specific routine to help them let go, relax, and get comfortable before approaching the next pitch.

How can you use your 'Inside the Zone' image to help you?

_____

_____

_____

 Workout 9
Mental Point

Everything happens twice. First, you see it in your mind, and then on the diamond. Create the atmosphere around what your peak performance on the ball field would look like; imagine the sounds, sights, and smells of your desired goals.

Dream On!
How Imagery Can Help You Win

What the Pros Are Saying

"Throughout the entire spring training, every night before I pitched, I'd imagine throwing all my pitches- fastball, change-up, curveball, to right-handers, to left-handers…. During that spring, I ended up pitching 20 consecutive scoreless innings."

> — **Bob Tewksbury,** Boston Red Sox Sport Psychology Coach, *Know The Power of Mental Imagery*, February 2017

"I envisioned what the game was going to look like and what my at-bats were going to look like. When I got in the box, I had already been there. I had already done it. I'm comfortable. I had seen it…. I'd imagine fastball away, just taking it…. Fastball away… Shooting it the other way. Fastball middle, down or up, fastball right there…. Boom…. I'd just imagine low line drives. Fastball in…. Boom…. Homerun."

> — **Eric Byrnes,** Former 10 Year Major League Outfielder, *Brian Cain's Peak Performance Podcast*, January 2017

Key Principles
1. Feel it, see it... do it!
2. If you can see it, you can do it.

Dream On!

What images come to mind when you hear the phrases "Imagine if…" or "Remember a time…?" For most baseball players, these words kick-start a flashback to a certain situation or moment during a game. Can you remember a time when you turned on an inside fastball, and drove it with authority for a double, in the gap? If you are really in-tune with yourself, you can hear the sound of the ball as it leaves the bat, and you can see the outfielders' backs as they chase the ball to the wall. The concept of visualization is essentially creating a mental picture of the situation unfolding. However, unlike memories, imagery occurs before the ump yells out "play ball". Hank Aaron once said, "You visualize pitches. You see it in your head; I used to play every pitcher in my mind before I went to the ballpark …"

This workout will highlight the different aspects of imagery: What is imagery in baseball? Who is using it? When can it be used? How can it be used? And how can it help you improve your performance on the field?

I often employ imagery as a key mental skill with my players. The most important component when beginning imagery is that the player is relaxed, and in a calm state of awareness.

What is imagery? Imagery is the purposeful act of rehearsing a task mentally with the intent of learning it. When a player uses imagery, he is creating a blueprint of his performance. It incorporates all of the senses: visual, kinesthetic, auditory, tactile, and olfactory. Additionally, it involves imagination, emotion, feelings, and moods. Essentially, the idea is to use your imagination to create or recreate a situation in the future, which will help you prepare for any possible scenario. With two outs and the go-ahead run on second, a pitcher may visualize himself making the perfect sequence of pitches to strikeout the hitter and get out of the jam.

Who uses imagery? Successful athletes do. I suspect you have even used imagery without knowing it—it's almost impossible not to have done so at some point. Have you ever imagined receiving a present, eating your favorite food, or going out with a friend? Have you ever studied for a test where you ran scenarios through your mind, planning out the best way to solve a problem? Most players use imagery in their day-to-day life without even knowing it. Imagine what would happen if you incorporated it into your day-to-day baseball practice with intention? If you're like most players, it will be beneficial.

When can imagery be used? Imagery can be used to practice certain tweaks or mechanical adjustments that players are trying to incorporate into their game. Maybe a hitter wants to learn a leg kick to generate more power and torque in their swing, or a pitcher wants to learn a new pitch and the arm motion associated with it. It can also be used to prepare for a situation that is likely to happen during each game. Maybe this includes pitching in front of a sold-out crowd at Minute Maid Park during the World Series. Houston Astros pitcher, Brad Peacock, picked up the first save of his entire career in Game 3 of the 2017 Fall Classic. He said, "When I was out there a couple of times, I got the chills from the crowd noise." Imagery prepared him to pitch in that type of situation with confidence, rather than allow the crowd's noise and the pressure of the situation to hinder his ability to perform.

Imagery can be used when you're unable to practice or play. Take Chicago Cubs outfielder Kyle Schwarber, who at the beginning of the 2016 season, tore his ACL in a horrific outfield collision. Without taking a single at-bat for the rest of the season, he made a miraculous comeback to be a part of the Cubs' unbelievable World Series victory, hitting over .400 at the plate for the series. A team source of the Cubs stated, "One thing Schwarber did was just sit in the cage. He'd watch pitches. He'd work with some of the guys doing pens, just to watch the spin." Kyle Scwarber himself said, "I set up a pitching machine for fastballs, sliders, and curveballs where I could just stand at the plate in a batter's box and watch these pitches go, just so I can see it and train my eyes all over again."

How can imagery be used? Picture a baseball player whose game you admire and would like to emulate. Specifically identify the characteristics, and attributes of that player that make him unique, and what you as a player would look like playing with these attributes. For example, take Hall of Fame pitcher Greg Maddux's command, Hall of Fame outfielder Ted Williams' plate discipline, and of Hall of Fame and all-time leader in stolen bases champion Ricky Henderson's speed on the bases, or maybe Hall of Fame infielder Ozzie Smith's fielding abilities. Visualize yourself playing with all the attributes you believe make a great player. You will become empowered as you see yourself playing with confidence, as each aspect of the game you are envisioning is what you believe peak potential looks like.

Players can also imagine specific situations by imagining the feelings, and emotions, of what a given situation would look and feel like, and then imagine making the proper adjustments for a positive outcome to occur.

How to get comfortable using imagery help you to improve your performance? It's easy, practice imagery five minutes a day, you will become more comfortable with the skill or situation.

Dream On!

WORKOUT

Self-Guided Imagery Script (instructions: read the script slowly, and notice what you experience as you read the words)

Find a comfortable position... just be aware of the sounds around you, just taking them in... Notice your breathing... and just observe its natural rhythm... No need to judge yourself, your thoughts or your feelings... just notice them for the moment... let them float by... allowing yourself this moment of quiet... You may begin to notice your body slowing down... feeling your body unwind... just let it unfold... observe this natural pendulum...

Now, would it be okay to turn your attention inward... I wonder if you can take yourself to a special place... a place you feel comfortable and secure... a place we will call Inside Your Zone... in this place... you're relaxed... it can be a place you have visited before... or a place you can only can go via your imagination... or it can be a place in your body, or even a feeling somewhere deep inside... that brings comfort... peace... it can be a combination of all these things... or anything... know one thing... this is your zone... and no one else's... As you look around... notice the surroundings... notice the smell... notice the feel... let it unfold... notice the sounds... sights... smells... or even tastes...

With this feeling of being inside your zone... shift your attention to the baseball diamond... a field of your choice... just notice what you see... let it unfold... in front of you... bring your awareness to a time you played great on the field... a time you did your best... be aware of the experience... feel it unfold... notice your energy... and your confidence... from inside YOUR zone...

What's it like to do your best... put it all on the line... play from your heart... would it be okay to stay with this feeling... even make some space for it... just notice what happens...

Now, gently bring attention back to your breathing... know you can go back to Your zone... any time you want... keep in mind you have the super player inside... you have the energy inside... use it... tap into it...

When you are ready... slowly bring yourself back... be aware of what your feet feel like touching the floor... notice the sounds around you...now slowly begin to bring yourself back to the present moment.

How do you feel now?_____

_____

_____

_____

_____

_____

_____

_____

Ryan Sliwak:
Fruits are a result of the roots.

It all starts with my family.
Love you guys!

Check out athletehumanity.com
and @athletehumanity.

High school ball at Wantagh

College ball at UMBC

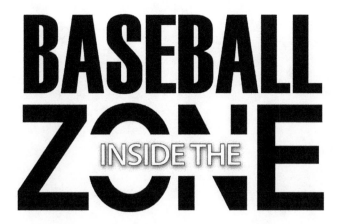

Section 2

PRE-GAME WORKOUTS

Workout 10: OMG... I'm Nervous! *Five Ways to Work Through Pre-Game Jitters*...............65

Workout 11: How to Play in the Moment: *It's as Easy as Breathing*...................71

Workout 12: Field Awareness: *Playing With Your Mental Positioning System*....................77

Workout 13: Why Can't I Play Games Like Practice? *Five Reasons This Happens*...............83

Workout 14: Concentrate! *Focus on What You Can Control*................................89

Workout 15: Rituals That Work: *Plan and Prepare for Success*.........................95

Workout 16: Stay Positive! *Seven Questions That Will Improve Your Game*......................101

Pre-Game Workouts

Can you remember a time you wanted to do something?
But, you were scared to "just let go" and "go for it?"

Imagine this…life is an ocean and you're a surfer.
At first you're afraid to get into the water.

Finally you go in and begin to trust the ocean.
Wading further out, going with the flow…

You realize, when you allow,
It starts to get easier; the water carries you.

Once you become comfortable with the ocean,
You look ahead; decide which waves to ride.
Steering away from trouble, rocks and other surfers.
Choosing the best way
While still going with the flow…

By Rob Polishook

Workout 10
Mental Point

Nervousness is not bad, nervousness is not good. Nervousness just is... Accept it and it usually dissolves away...

OMG... I'm Nervous!
Five Ways to Work Through Pre-Game Jitters

What the Pros Are Saying

"Everyone has 'em, everyone has butterflies. If you don't feel them, I guess you're not human."
> — **Derek Jeter,** World Series MVP and 5x World Series Champion, *Game one of the 2009 playoffs, Channel 5, Oct. 6th, 2009*

"A baseball game is simply a nervous breakdown broken down into nine innings"
> — **Earl Wilson,** Former Major League Pitcher, *Baseball Almanac*

"Never let the fear of striking out get in your way."
> — **Babe Ruth,** *Baseball Almanac*

Key Principles
1. Everyone gets nervous.
2. If you're not nervous, you're not human.
3. Nerves are a great indicator of passion!

OMG... I'm Nervous!

BZZZZ, BZZZZZ. It's usually a weekend, in my world. I may have just finished watching a morning segment of ESPN or MLB network. All is relaxed while I drink my morning coffee. Yet for the baseball player on the other end of my buzzing cell phone, his world is anything but calm. Butterflies are fluttering through his stomach, his head may be spinning with possible performance outcomes, and self-doubt is creeping in.

The player wonders what is happening to him. Perhaps a pitcher is preparing to face a deep lineup, or an infielder is coming off a game with multiple errors. It's at this very moment our paths connect with a *BZZZZZ* on the cell phone, or a short but direct text message. It's always the same as I listen intently or scroll down my phone: I hear or read, "I'm nervous—what do I do?"

As a mental training coach, this is probably the most commonly asked question I receive. As many ballplayers who have experienced such jitters can attest, it's usually not the nervousness itself that presents a problem, but all the thoughts that accompany it, such as "Why am I nervous?" or "What happens if I'm still this nervous at-bat, in the field?" This then sets off another negative spiral, and the player's natural nervousness turns into a far more debilitating anxiety.

In light of this, I want to share five ideas with which the nervous player can gain some perspective over what's happening and be able to better manage, and work through excessive nervousness.

1. It's okay to be nervous—it's perfectly normal and natural. In fact, even the top players in the world admit to nervousness. In a sit-down interview with Silver Slugger Award winner, Anthony Rizzo, he talked about the type of nervousness he felt prior to Game 7 of the 2016 World Series; "It was nerve-racking, I was trying to sleep, and whenever I shut my eyes, you got the good things and the bad things. Don't miss that pop up. Don't strikeout with bases loaded. But then there's the good things, like hitting the home run, or driving in the big hit." This self-acceptance of nerves is actually the way to manage the situation. The top players don't fight the tension; rather they accept it, as "something inside of them is nervous." How many of you have tried to resist a feeling or a thought? What happens? It usually gets bigger and bigger, and instead looms in your mind.

2. Nervousness is a sign that you care. Nervousness isn't bad, nervousness isn't good—it simply exists. It's your own unique way of reacting to different situations throughout a game. 3x American League Manager of the Year, Buck Showalter, stated, "We all get nervous out there, but we just have a different way of hiding it... it's ok to be that way." There are always two sides to everything, but when you're nervous, usually you only focus on the negative aspects of how you feel. As a hitter, you feel anxious. The anxiousness builds, the game begins to speed up, and you wiggle the bat in your fingertips a little faster. However, what's the other side? Aren't you also *excited, challenged, aware*; maybe even *focused* because you have a great opportunity in front of you, and you're in that big spot late in the game that you've imagined yourself being in since you were a little kid, playing ball in your backyard? Remember: embrace this challenge. Your nerves are simply a by-product of the thrill.

3. If you are nervous, who else is? When a player is nervous, his focus is usually entirely on himself. In other words, he is not seeing the entire picture, rather just a small piece of it. 5x All-Star and 2x Gold Glove winner, Troy Tulowitzki, said, "Some hitters see hitting with runners on base as a pressure situation for themselves. It helps me to focus on how the pressure is really on the pitcher and the defense." Don't forget about your opponent! The team in the other dugout accounts for 50% of the puzzle. In fact, that pitcher, fielder, or batter wearing different colored pinstripes, and sharing the same diamond as you, are just as nervous as you are, perhaps even more so!

4. What's the worst that can happen? Hall of Fame Manager, Casey Stengel, once said, "There are three things you can do in a baseball game: you can win, you can lose, or it can rain." In baseball, you succeed or you fail, but even the greatest hitter of all-time, Ted Williams, knew that "baseball is the only endeavor where a man can succeed three times out of ten and be considered a good performer." So… what's the worst that can happen? In the game of baseball, you are going to fail much more than you are going to succeed, and that is what makes this sport so unique! But as Hall of Fame outfielder Ken Griffey Jr. put it, "You lose, you smile, and you come back the next day. You win, you smile, and you come back the next day."

5. Why am I nervous? When I ask this question to players, they usually say it's because "I want to win," or "I don't know how I'm going to do," or "I'm not sure how good the other team's lineup or pitcher is." What's important to understand is that the player's focus is distracted. Their focus is on something they cannot control, which is winning (the result). More so, they are focusing on another uncontrollable, which is their opponent. Sometimes a hitter is more focused on how the other team's pitcher looks in the bullpen during warm-ups, rather than what he needs to do to make sure his mechanics and swing are game ready. With a focus on the uncontrollable, there is little time to focus on what they need to do to perform their best.

Nervousness is a natural emotion and is part of who you are. The problem is not the nervousness that a player experiences. The issue is the negative reaction from these nerves. The next time you are nervous, refer to the five above techniques to help you play your best game.

OMG... I'm Nervous!

WORKOUT

What's important to understand is that everyone gets nervous. Like Jeter says, "If you're not nervous, you're probably not human!" You're nervous because you care, and you want to be successful on the diamond… certainly understandable! Further, if you're nervous… I bet the other team is also. So… maybe it's okay to be nervous!

Remember a game where you were nervous, but everything worked out great in the end. Describe it.

_____

_____

_____

What where you feeling?

_____

_____

What did you notice about the nerves as the game went on?

_____

_____

_____

What would your experience be if you didn't judge the nervousness as good or bad?

_____

_____

_____

Baseball Inside the Zone™

Using the principles from this chapter, what could you say to yourself to manage the nervousness?

_____

_____

_____

How could you reframe your nerves in a way that could help you?

1. _____

2. _____

3. _____

How would doing the above help you in tense situations?

_____

_____

_____

Look out into the ocean...
Simply observe your breath...
Notice what you experience in
your body...

When you're nervous in a game,
it can be helpful to bring up a
time when you were calm.
This mini-second break can help
calm and reset your system.

Workout 11
Mental Point

Bring your attention to your breath. For a moment... simply notice the sound of your breath, then notice the feel of your breath, then notice the rhythm of your breath. Just be curious...

How to Play in the Moment:
It's as Easy as Breathing

What the Pros Are Saying

"Remember your breathing. Don't worry about the results. Stay in the moment. Prepare to get a hit."

— **Evan Longoria,** 3x Gold Glove and Silver Slugger Winner, *Bleacher Report* 2017

"One of the physical things that happens is you take shorter breaths and your breathing is kind of abnormal when there's high pressure, and so you just have to learn to notice when that's happening and then take a second to relax your breathing and kind of control it a little bit, take deep breaths, and make sure that you slow down."

— **Michael Conforto,** All-Star Outfielder, *New York Post* 2015

"There's a process and preparation. You start by breathing, getting your mind into that mode where you're going to compete"

— **Jose Bautista,** 6x All-Star and Silver Slugger Award winner, *Sportsnet.com*

"When you're breathing, you always got a chance"

— **Joe Panik,** All-Star and Gold Glove winner, *MLB Network* , October 11th, 2016

Key Principles

1. Your breath is always in the present moment.
2. Focus on your breath—calm on the inside, aware on the outside.
3. Notice your breath and let go of everything else.

How to Play in the Moment

If you're reading this workout, you're breathing. Interestingly, the majority of us take this subtle automatic action for granted. Why is this? Breathing is regulated by our autonomic nervous system. This means it happens without our conscious awareness. This is probably fortunate, because during games many of us would be too busy to remember to breathe! By bringing your awareness to your breath, it will calm you, slow the game down, and help you reach that state of mind where you are focused, centered, and relaxed.

Our mind is usually in two places: the past and the future. When our mind is in the past, we are usually conjuring up thoughts, feelings, and images of memories that have stayed with us. An example might be thinking about our last at-bat, an error in the field we made last inning, or missing our spot and letting up a big hit. When our mind is in the future, we are usually focused on expectations of what we think is going to happen. While in the field, you may be thinking about what adjustments you need to make for your next at-bat. As a pitcher, maybe you are focusing on the hitter on-deck. How many of us have done that and gone on to make an error or mistake? These scenarios are mental traps! Both scenarios fall into the realm of what an athlete cannot control. Baseball players can only control what they need to do to prepare for the next pitch, so that's where the focus must be.

Fortunately, our body and breath are always in the present time. It is said that the 'present' is named as such because being in the present is like a gift, like a hanging curveball down the heart of the plate! The breath is one of the greatest gifts we have. When this tool is used properly, it can serve as an anchor, helping us to stay centered and focused. Simply bringing our attention to the natural rhythm of our breath can take our focus away from stressful situations, and connect to our body, rhythm, and timing. Try this experiment. Ask yourself, "Am I breathing?" Sit silently for 30 seconds and notice what happens.

The following three breathing practices can be used to guide you to stay centered, focused, and in a state of calm awareness. Practice them off the diamond for a few minutes each day. Then, use the one that feels best for you between pitches or innings, or any time you find yourself losing focus.

1. Unguided Breathing: The object here is to bring your attention to your natural breathing, wherever it is, at the present moment. Just be aware of one of the following senses: sound, feel, or rhythm. How does your breath sound? How does it feel? Notice its rhythm at that moment. Don't try to change anything or judge it. Just observe its natural organic pace. You may even prompt yourself by asking, "Am I breathing?" What you will usually notice after five or ten seconds is that your breath will slow down, and so will the pace of the game.

2. Word Association Breathing: As you breathe in, say to yourself the word *relaxation, slow, or patient*, and imagine what it would feel like to be relaxed. Then, exhale, and say the word anxious, or fast, and imagine what it would feel like to let go of the anxiousness at the plate or on the mound, or the overwhelming feeling when the game seems to speed up on you. Visualize tension leaving your body, and feel your internal clock at just the right speed. You may make up your own words to suit the situation. However, the key is to inhale what you want, and exhale what you do not need.

3. Rhythmic Breathing: The object here is to breathe to an established rhythm that feels best for you. What's important with this exercise is that you find a pattern that works for you and stick to it. Try inhaling to the count of three, hold your breath for two counts, and then exhale to the count of four beats. When a pitcher is locating all his pitches, and working effectively to get outs, we say he's found his rhythm; the idea here is for you to find your rhythm using your breath! What feels best? Be creative and experiment with your own rhythms. Have fun!

Whichever breathing practice you're using, once you're centered with a soft focus on your breath, allow your attention to expand and take in everything around you. Be aware of sounds, sights, and even thoughts as they pass by. Metaphorically, this breathing practice is similar to the eye of a hurricane: you are calm on the inside but very active on the outside. Former National League Manager of the Year Award winner, Terry Collins, stated, "The idea is to slow down. Slow. Down. Slow the heart rate down; slow the thinking process; slow it down. Instead of rushing, take a second, take a breath, and assess what's going on." Slowing down the game with our breath allows you to respond to each pitch, inning, and game with clarity. Remember: clarity creates consistency, and consistency is the name of the game!

It's easy playing in the moment when your having fun.

How to Play in the Moment

WORKOUT

It's as Easy as Breathing!

Breathing is regulated by our autonomic nervous system: It happens without thinking (fortunately!). By bringing attention to our breath, we can connect to our ever-present body.

Below are the three different breathing exercises that can be used between pitches or innings, or anytime you need to slow your internal clock down, change your focus, and calm down.

Unguided Breathing Exercise

Start this exercise by asking yourself... Am I breathing? Then, simply notice your in and out breaths. One breath at a time, notice the sound, feel, and then rhythm—whichever sense you connect best with. Just be aware of that and be curious. Notice how you may let go of everything else as you do this.

Word Association Breathing Exercise

List characteristics, attributes, or emotions you would want to <u>breathe in</u> and <u>breathe out</u>.

<u>Breathe in:</u>	<u>Breathe out:</u>
Patience	Fear

Now, as you breathe in, imagine what it would feel like to breathe patience in, to feel patience flowing through. Then imagine what it would look like to breathe anxiousness out, and visualize the anxiousness separating, and leaving your mind and body. Do the same thing with the words that feel right for you.

Rhythmic Breathing Exercise

Breathe in and count how many seconds the breath is... Then, notice a possible pause, then breathe out and notice how many seconds it is. Discover your rhythm. What feels best?

Beats in:_____

Beats holding breath:_____

Beats out:_____

Summary

These three breathing exercises are intended to help ballplayers slow down, change focus, and stay in the present moment of each pitch. Experiment with each exercise to discover which ones you can incorporate into your pre-, during-, and post-game routines.

Look out this plane window:
- Just be curious
- Simply observe your breath
- Notice what you experience

Workout 12
Mental Point

When you're on the field, don't take a shortcut. Objectively assess what is happening each pitch so that you can make the best possible adjustment to reach your goal.

Field Awareness:
Playing With Your Mental Positioning System

What the Pros Are Saying

"It starts with having a game plan, having an approach with your early work. When I go into early work, I say, 'What am I going to accomplish?' I'm not going into the cage just to take 100 swings. I have a routine and I'm sticking to it. In the game, I go to the plate with the game plan against the pitcher I'm going to face."
> — **Steve Lombardozzi,** MLB Utility Player, *MLB.com*, May 31st, 2012

"If you know yourself and are able to make adjustments, you will improve as a player and have the potential to help those around you improve, because you understand them."
> — **David Ross,** 2x World Series Champion, <u>Teammate: My Journey in Baseball and A World Series for the Ages</u>.

"When you divide your focus, you're dividing everything that you have. You're not putting everything that you could have put into that pitch, into that location, so you're going to miss. That's why people fail -- because they broke focus. That's something I've learned over the years: if players break a focus, they break their success for that pitch."
> — **Rajai Davis,** MLB Outfielder, *CBSsports.com* Feb 9th, 2017

Key Principles
1. The process begins with an end goal in mind.
2. You are where you are...Stay in the moment.
3. Change starts with awareness.

Field Awareness

Let's flash back a few years to a time when people read maps to determine how to reach a destination. Three steps were necessary: first, you needed to be aware of your current location; second, you needed to know where you wanted to go; and third, you needed to plan the most efficient route to reach your desired destination.

In today's day and age, everyone has a global positioning system (GPS) in their phone. Certainly, the GPS app has made it easier to reach your destination. All that is necessary is to input the destination and *voilà*—the GPS tells you where to go. There need be little awareness of where you currently are, and no thinking or planning is necessary. So, what does this have to do with baseball? A lot, stay with me.

On the diamond, we can't turn to our GPS to reach our goals. Thankfully, all players have a similar, yet superior tool of cognition. This tool is what I refer to as the MPS, or *Mental Positioning System*. The MPS is a human machine, run by the strongest computer in the universe—not an electronic device, but our own brain. It is activated by awareness. It requires us to examine the same three points we needed to ask when using a map: where we are at this exact point in time, where do we want to end up, and what the necessary steps are in order to reach that goal.

A mentally sound player can employ his MPS in both practice and games.

Activated by awareness, the player's MPS can tell him whether he is using the most ideal approach for the situation, what adjustments need to be made mechanically and mentally, and lastly, what is the end goal. This system will help you identify where you are, the result you are looking for, and how to properly plan to get there.

Some players may use their MPS more than others and consequently reap the benefits, while others may take the shortcuts that our GPS uses. For example, many players simply say, "I want to win"—in other words they input the destination like with a GPS. However, as Hall of Famer Frank Thomas said, "There is no shortcut to success." Taking the shorter route often will result in inconsistent performances on the field, on the mound, and at the plate.

During a game, it is imperative to be aware, and realize that each situation changes pitch by pitch. Furthermore, it's key to understand tendencies and patterns of pitchers, hitters, and teams. Now, knowing yourself as a player, you must determine what you are trying to accomplish, and what necessary steps need to be made in order to achieve this.

MVP Award winner and 2x Silver Slugger Award winner, Josh Donaldson, said, "I think, for some people, it gets a little cloudy because they don't necessarily understand themselves or understand the situation of the game. That's where the experience and everything plays in. You have to know yourself and know your ability."

To use your MPS properly in practice, here are some questions you can ask yourself in practice:

- Where am I now, with regard to a particular skill?

- Where do I want to be in a certain amount of time?

- To get there, what do I have to do/what will it take?

- Am I willing to put in the effort to do this? Who can help me?

- How will I know when I reach this goal?

To use your MPS in games, ask yourself these questions:

- What is happening at this moment?

- What do I want to happen?

- What adjustments do I need to make?

- How would the situation change if I made these adjustments?

- What's one adjustment I can make now?

Remember, when you're on the field, don't take the shortcut by trying to use your GPS. Tune into your internal MPS and trust yourself to objectively assess what is happening each pitch. This will help you make the best possible adjustments to reach your goal. You will find that using your mind to change the course of different situations throughout a game is one of the most fulfilling experiences in baseball.

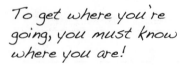

To get where you're going, you must know where you are!

Field Awareness

WORKOUT

You can't get somewhere without being aware and knowing where you are! Try completing the following three steps in regards to a goal or challenge.

Describe where you currently are in regards to a goal or challenge.

_____

_____

_____

_____

_____

_____

Describe where you want to be.

_____

_____

_____

_____

_____

_____

Knowing where you are now and where you want to be... what three things do you need to do to get there?

1. _____

2. _____

3. _____

Workout 13
Mental Point

A baseball player must always remember that each moment of adversity or prosperity, in a game or in practice, is all part of a journey in which continual improvement is the ultimate goal.

Why can't I play games like practice?
Five reasons this happens

What the Pros Are Saying

"Practice… It's a time to create and foster good habits. The guys who do it, and do it right, are the ones who are more successful. There aren't any outs in practice… It's a practice of habit and discipline."

> — **Chili Davis,** 3x World Series Champion and 3x All-Star, *ESPN.com*, September 11th 2014

"We can try to prepare and gain confidence through practice, but when you get out there, it's a whole different dynamic. The mental side is as important or more important than the mechanics."

> — **Paul Molitor**, 4x Silver Slugger Award Winner and World Series MVP and Champion, *ESPN.com*, September 11th, 2014

"How good can you be? I don't know how good you can be, do you? But one thing's for sure. If you have faith, courage, and trust in yourself , you will find out. You may exceed your wildest expectations."

> — **Rob Polishook,** M.A., C.P.C., Mental Training Coach

Key Principles

1. Fact: a game is different than practice.
2. The more you need to win, the less you will.
3. Every player feels the pressure to perform in the clutch; it's how you react to it.

Rob Polishook

Why can't I play games like practice?

"**W**hy do I play better in practice than in games?" It's probably the second most asked question I hear from players, exceeded only by some variation of "I'm nervous, what do I do?" Sometimes this question comes out as a defiant statement, where the player stubbornly says, "If I pitched like I did in my bullpen session, I would have thrown a complete game shutout and got the win" or, "If I swung as well as I did during my cage work, I'd be able to catch just about any pitch on the barrel and drive it." Interestingly, that statement is usually true. Yet practice and games are different from each other in intensity and pressure.

In practice, whether in the cage, during fielding drills, or throwing a side pen, we are competing against ourselves to evolve our own game. When we compete during a game, our opponent is simply there to add another dimension to our development. In fact, the opposing players can be thought of as partners. They are there to help you improve, to make you uncomfortable, and help you learn from adversity.

2x World Series Champion manager, Joe Maddon, said, "It's really important to be uncomfortable. If you become a comfortable person, I think that subtracts growth from the equation. I think that if you remain somewhat uncomfortable, you'll continue to grow. You don't want to become stagnant. You don't become complacent, set in your ways. On every level… Remain uncomfortable. I think that's a really positive word.

"Games should not be solely categorized as wins and losses but evaluated in ways that help us grow from them. As said in previous workouts, the game of baseball revolves around constantly making adjustments. Each game and each practice, represents an opportunity to be aware, fine-tune your ability, and adjust to reach your goals.

The remainder of this workout will explore five key reasons why players perform differently in practice and during games.

1. Loss of Focus: Throughout each game, a player's focus is usually on the outcome, rather than the present moment. When a player focuses on the result of an at-bat, or a pitch they just threw, they are focusing on something they cannot control. When they focus on the present, they are in a problem-solving mode, and they are able to evaluate, and understand what areas of their game need to be adjusted in preparation for the next pitch. In practice, the focus is usually on the process: finding your hand slot at the plate, working through the baseball in the field, and experimenting with a new pitch. During a game, the key is to let go of the result, and get back to focusing on the process.

2. Too Many Expectations: In games, many baseball players expect to square up a pitch every at-bat. Some players show little tolerance when they just miss a pitch, and pop it straight up. Conversely, a player usually expects to make mistakes in practice, and uses his mistakes as a learning tool. In fact, they are a vital part of development. In essence, the player is allowing himself to fail, and evaluating how his mistakes are putting him in a better position to reach his goals. Even World Series Champion, 3x Silver Slugger Award winner and 3 Gold Glove winner, Mark Teixeira, said, "Baseball is a game of failure." Players should expect to make mistakes in games. Rather than channeling their energy into the ball they misplayed, or the location they missed, they should focus on the process of adjustments, just as they would during practice reps. This is a vital part of playing and competing on a consistent level every game. Remember there is an E column on the scoreboard for a reason: errors and mistakes are a part of the game.

3. Poor Time Management: In practice, baseball players sometimes rush through drills, allowing little time to incorporate routines, or even to discuss with their coach the purpose and intentions of the drill. As a player, take ownership of the time between pitches and practice drills to simulate an in-game situation. Practice your routines and rituals that you do between pitches. If, after each swing, you step out of the box, take a deep breath, and adjust your batting gloves a certain way, do that in practice. This built-in similarity to game-like situations will help players bridge the gap between practice and game.

4. Nerves: Players are rarely nervous in practice. This is because they are not judging themselves, nor is anyone else. During the game, players often find themselves bringing their attention to the judgment of the fans, the other team, etc. As a result, they begin to worry about the result of their on-field execution, focusing on uncontrollable factors of the game. It's also important to remember that if you are nervous, so is the opposing team. Players on every level of baseball get nervous. Think about 3x All-Star and Gold Glove winner, Anthony Rizzo's famous sound bite from Game 7 of the 2016 World Series, "I can't control my nerves right now, I'm emotional, I am an emotional wreck. I am in a glass case of emotion." It's not a matter of avoiding nerves, but learning to accept them.

5. Trying to Impress Others: In practice, players focus on improving and performing the drills that their coaches are working on with them. During games, all of a sudden, others are watching. Playing time, scholarships, and contracts are all on the line. Players often lose focus on the game, and instead worry about impressing the people in the stands. Conversely, they start thinking about what aspects of their game they need to showcase in order to impress. This may include a pitcher overthrowing because he is only focusing on lighting up the radar gun. A player may also worry about criticism from a parent or coach for not performing well against a less talented team. Think about a hitter who pops up 3 consecutive at-bats to the infield, because the pitcher is throwing below average velocity, and he is trying to hit a homerun. In all cases, the player's focus is no longer on the present. It is key for players to recognize when they lose their focus and refocus on the present moment.

Why can't I play games like practice?

WORKOUT

In baseball, each game and practice present an opportunity to self-evaluate, and make the proper adjustments based on your own assessments of each pitch. They represent the part of the process where you truly come to understand yourself as a player, develop, and improve. So, while playing a game is different from practice, what would happen if you viewed it as practice? A place to learn and get better?

List three things that you focus on in practice...

1. _____

2. _____

3. _____

When you focus on these things, what do you notice?

_____

_____

_____

List three things that you focus on in games...

1. _____

2. _____

3. _____

When you focus on these things, what do you notice?

_____

_____

_____

_____

What is the main difference?

_____

_____

_____

_____

What things would make sense to let go of when you play games?

_____

_____

_____

_____

What things that you focus on in practice would be helpful if you focused on them in game situations?

_____

_____

_____

_____

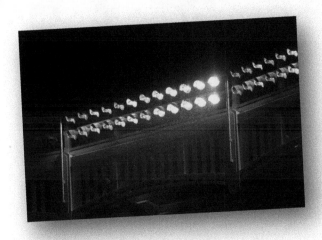

It's show time when the lights go on!

Workout 14
Mental Point

All players will inevitably lose focus. Rather than doubting or getting angry at yourself, simply accept and re-focus. This non-judgmental approach will help the player reframe and stay in the present.

Concentrate!
Focus on What You Can Control

What the Pros Are Saying

"You can't control what happens after the ball leaves the bat, but you can control what happens before that. You can control your lower half, hands, and front elbow during your swing."

> — **Sean Casey,** 3x All-Star and Cincinnati Reds Hall of Famer, *Baseball Network.* March 5th, 2018

"Baseball is so difficult, and so much of this game is out of our control. A hitter is measured by "hits", which are largely uncontrollable. Pitchers are measured by "wins", which are largely uncontrollable. We worry about umpires, the field, the mound, the bat, and the fans too often. We concentrate on too much that is out of our control. Just control what you can control."

> — **Chad Moeller,** Former MLB Catcher, *Chadmoellerbaseball.com*, August 20th, 2013

"You've got to be in control of yourself before you can be in control of your performance."

> — **Ken Ravizza**, Sports Psychologist, *15 Critical Questions on the Mental Game of Baseball*, Feb 27th, 2018

Key Principles
1. The outcome is not something you can control.
2. Focusing on uncontrollables creates tightness.
3. Everyone loses focus. Recognize when this happens and re-focus.

Concentrate!

We've all heard the phrase, "He got caught napping!" It happens when a baserunner loses his focus on the base paths and gets picked off. It's happened to us all. One moment you are concentrating and everything feels smooth, relaxed, and in control. The next moment you seemingly find yourself walking back to the dugout because your mind was in the past or looking ahead to the future.

Or perhaps you have experienced this a different way: You're on the mound late in the game with your team up a run, with a man on third and 2 outs. The only thought that is running through your head is that after this out, you only have one more inning to get through. You begin to press, your heart rate goes up, and you begin rushing through your delivery. Next thing you know, you've walked the next two batters, and the bases are loaded. You are left to wonder how your concentration strayed from "one pitch at a time" to seemingly everywhere except the present!

Concentration is one of the most important and misunderstood mental skills in a baseball player's skill set. 8x All-Star and 2x Cy Young Award winner, Roy Halladay, said, "It's what helped get me where I need to be…. readjust and get back to having focus on singular pitches, working counts, and simplifying." Concentrate on the task at hand and focus on the next pitch.

Sports Psychologist Harvey Dorfman said, "To focus on matters beyond our control is to misdirect energy, waste time, and doom us to frustration and failure." This implies that an athlete may be concentrating, but if it's on the wrong thing, it only serves to hinder his performance on the diamond. Many common phrases said on the baseball field revolve around either a coach or parent prompting a player to concentrate or focus! The athlete probably *is* concentrating, but maybe not on the right thing. This oft-repeated advice is not specific enough. For example, a player may be reflecting on the previous play in the field or anticipating getting up to bat in a certain situation later in the game, while the coach is prodding them to concentrate on what's happening on the next pitch.

My mentor, Dr. Alan Goldberg, defines concentration as the choice to focus on what you can control, and let go of what you can't control. Think about a time you found yourself focusing on something you had no control over, like the outcome of an at-bat? What did it do to your anxiety level? How did it affect your concentration as the pitch was about to be delivered? Focusing on something we cannot control almost always clouds our minds, inhibits performance, and hinders our abilities to make proper adjustments. Conversely, focusing on something you *can* control, will yield more confidence, and sense of control.

There is a helpful strategy which players can use to help them concentrate on what they can control before each game. Try this exercise: on the left side of a sheet of paper, list what you can control during a game and label it "controllables." Your list might include preparation, staying positive, adjustments, breathing, and how you react to calls or situations. On the right side of the paper, list what you are unable to control—such as the weather, field conditions, the outcome, etc. Simply by labeling what you can and cannot control, you will have increased your awareness of where you want your focus to be. Without this awareness, the athlete will continue to focus on the wrong thing. During each game, the act of re-focusing is just as important as maintaining your focus in the first place.

World Series winning manager, Joe Maddon, said, "Self-awareness is really what it comes down to. If there are 30,000 people yelling, and there are guys on base, sometimes you get caught up in all the emotion. I want our players to be able to be self-aware of what's required in the moment."

In summary, when viewing concentration through the lens of what you can control and what you cannot, it becomes much more manageable to play at the best of your ability that day, on the field. A player can benefit from learning to re-focus effectively rather than attempting to maintain being dialed in at all times. In fact, letting go will perpetuate even stronger concentration by providing a more relaxed focus, and will lead to more consistent performances.

For the Love of the Game:
Bert Strane

Concentrate!

WORKOUT

Concentration: kan(t)·sen·'tra·shen: noun, 1964: the act or process of concentrating; the state of being concentrated; especially: direction of attention of a single object. B. to bring or direct towards a common object. To draw together and meet in a common center; to focus one's power, efforts or attention.

How would you define *concentration* in the context of sports?

_____

_____

_____

Inside the Zone definition of concentration: *The ability to focus on what is important, and let go of everything else.*

Translation:

> **The ability to focus** = The choice to focus
>
> **on what is important** = on what you can control
>
> **and let go of everything else** = and let go of what you can't control

New complete definition (write it in):

_____

_____

What percentage of the time in games do you concentrate on what you can control?

_____

And what percentage of the time in games do you concentrate on what you cannot control?

_____

Name a time during a game when you were concentrating on the right thing:

_____

_____

What was the result?

_____

_____

_____

Name a time during a game when you were concentrating on the wrong thing:

_____

_____

What was the result?

_____

_____

_____

Understanding this new definition of concentration, and the above, how could this change things for you?

_____

_____

_____

_____

_____

Workout 15
Mental Point

The evening before a game, or even hours before a game, it is important to stick to your rituals in order to put yourself in the best position to perform at your highest level.

Rituals That Work:
Plan and Prepare for Success

What the Pros Are Saying

"I go through my pre-game routines and make sure my mind is where it needs to be. This helps me focus on what I need to do in order to achieve my performance objectives. The difference between a good game and a bad game is your mental approach."
> — **Chase Utley,** 6x All-Star and 4x Silver Slugger Award Winner, *Sports Psychology Today*

"Some guys need to swing and swing. Other guys have one swing and say 'I'm good' and just walk out of the cage. Everyone knows guys who hit until they're sweating. Everybody is different. It's a comfort thing."
> — **Andrew McCutchen,** 5x All-Star and MVP Winner, *Batting Practice: Swings and Misses, ESPN.com*

Key Principles
1. Rituals help an athlete feel prepared.
2. Rituals create a baseline for consistency.
3. Rituals grant player's control.

Rituals That Work

You can't control the future, but you can prepare for it. This is where rituals come in to play. Baseball players are creatures of habit, and every player should develop a set of rituals that he feels are necessary to put himself in the best position to be successful. What can you do the night before your game, or even hours before the game that day? The answer is—a lot! It is important to understand that this is not the time to make technique changes. This is not the time to make a drastic adjustment in your stance or hitting philosophy, or radically tweak your pitching mechanics. Instead, this is the time to mentally prepare, and get ready for the next game.

Think of it this way—if you were a pilot, you would have a checklist of all the things you needed to double-check before takeoff. If you were a carpenter, you would "measure twice and cut once." The same goes for baseball! The main goal at this point is to be relaxed and present. The idea is to be mentally grounded so your instincts and skills can naturally take over during the game.

Pre-game rituals for each player vary immensely, ranging from watching film, eating specific meals at specific times, sleeping, or taking batting practice. Let's take batting practice for example. For most players, this a time each player has a unique ritual to get a great feel for their swing that day, so that they feel confident in the box at game. This could be taking 10 swings or taking 100 swings, or maybe a pull hitter specifically works on an opposite field approach. 3x MVP and 6x Silver Slugger Award winner, Albert Pujols, stated, "Whatever you bring to B.P. is what's going to show in the game." On the other hand, during the 2015 All-Star game, 6x All-Star and MVP Award winner, Bryce Harper, revealed in an interview, "I don't take B.P. I haven't taken B.P. in 4 months." Clearly, both players have very unique approaches to their pre-game rituals, yet each player is a generational talent. The common factor is that they have created a pre-game ritual and approach that mentally works for them. There is no uniform definition of what each player's pre-game rituals should look like. The following is a list of 5 suggestions, which you may choose to incorporate into your pre-game routine:

1. Pre-game Checklist and 'Altar': The evening before a game, or the morning of, lie out and pack whatever you are going to need to compete. My wife, Debbie, is a marathon runner and refers to this as "laying out her altar." It's her process to ensure she has everything that's necessary to compete, and that she won't have to run around last minute trying to find something on the day of her competition. Proper preparation also helps to ensure that on the day of the game, you are relaxed, as it eliminates the potential stress of completing another last-minute task. Items for the 'altar' might include a uniform, cleats, glove, batting gloves, bat, tape, arm sleeves, etc.

2. Sleep and Hydration: Hopefully, you have been getting enough sleep and hydrating yourself leading up to the game. However, it is imperative to get to bed early the evening before a game. Most adults need eight hours of sleep; however, kids may need ten hours. Plan this into your evening, and work backwards so you can bank enough sleep. When you make it to the big leagues and get drafted by the Red Sox, you can utilize their "Nap Room", a 145-foot room with beds built in the clubhouse specifically for players to take naps before games! I also always recommend hydrating leading up to the game and keeping water by your bed.

3. Pre-game Strategy: The night before or morning of a game, mentally go through your thoughts about the opponent, and develop an approach. For hitters and pitchers, this would include identifying opposing tendencies and creating a game plan on how to attack it. Lock it in, and then visualize yourself successfully performing the strategy in the game. As a batter, identify that a pitcher has a tendency to get ahead with a first pitch fastball. Visualize yourself looking for that fastball, getting that fastball, and jumping all over it with conviction. As a pitcher, recognize that a certain hitter gets anxious with runners in scoring position at the plate, and always tries to do too much. Adjust your pitch sequence to expose the batter's over-anxiousness at the plate and visualize yourself getting out of the situation successfully. It's key to understand that adversity usually rears its head during a game, be it a bad call, unruly fans, bad weather, or the like. Preparing for uncontrollable elements and visualizing how you will handle them under pressure will better prepare you to handle the situation when it occurs.

4. Stretch and Warm-Up: This step can be overlooked. It's important to stretch, not so much as something to do, but rather to "feel into" the stretch, noticing where you might be tight, and bringing extra attention to that area. Also bring your mental focus to the area you are stretching, and breath through it. Not only does this time help your body to relax and stay loose, but it also helps to center yourself, becoming aware and calm. Also, taking dry swings while mentally simulating an at-bat, or going out to your position and working on your lateral movement will help you simulate a strategy, engage different movements, and create a mental map of the field, and how it feels underneath your feet.

5. Chill: So often this step is ignored, yet, it is so helpful in achieving a relaxed, balanced mindset for the game. Just before a game is not the time to be concocting new strategies or devising drastic adjustments. Look at what 23x Gold Medalist Olympic swimmer, Michael Phelps, does before a race... nothing! He listens to his iPod, and just chills. He is relaxing his nervous system. When it's race time, he can give it 100%.

Utilize these five tactics to prepare for success. Remember from the goal setting workouts: players don't plan to fail, they fail to plan! Proper preparation and rituals can help you be ready for whatever happens.

Rituals That Work

WORKOUT

Pre-Match Checklist

A pilot, prior to take-off, will methodically go through a checklist to ensure the plane is properly equipped with the right supplies, and will run smoothly. Similarly, a mentally ready ballplayer will go through their essentials, and necessities, to ensure they are feeling comfortable and confident for their game. Improper preparation will immediately put you a step behind.

The first few items you cannot find in a baseball bag; they are intangible things that only you can control...

1. A good night's sleep the night leading up to the game (eight hours minimum).

2. Drink water leading up to the game, to hydrate your body.

3. A positive, problem-solving, happy attitude; that includes confidence in the adjustments and strategies that you implemented into your game plan for that game.

Bag Check:

1. _____ Back up glove (if you play more than one position, or simply have a backup glove)

2. _____ Batting gloves and helmet

3. _____ If you are a catcher: Mask/chest protector/shin guards/thumb guard

4. _____ Cleats

5. _____ Water/Sunflower seeds/Gum/Power Bar/ etc.

6. _____ Sunglasses

7. _____ Hat

8. _____ Arm bands/Tape/EvoShield/Leg Guard/Wristbands/Eye black/ etc.

9. _____ Extra baseballs

10. _____   Grips: Make sure you have extra grip tape with you—or if you are using a wood bat, pine tar

11. _____   Something that makes you smile

12. _____   Something that motivates you (See Workout 3: Your Big Why!)

13. _____   Pen or pencil, and notebook, to take notes about different batters and pitchers throughout the game.

14. _____   (Anything else?)

15. _____   _____

16. _____   _____

17. _____   _____

Looking out to the Galapagos Islands.

Great Darwin quote... How does it relate to your baseball game?

Workout 16
Mental Point

What if you could improve your game by simply asking yourself—and thoughtfully answering—a few questions? Would that be worth it to you?

Workout 16

Stay Positive!
Seven Questions That Will Improve Your Game

What the Pros Are Saying

"Being able to constantly tell yourself that you believe in yourself and what you're doing literally makes all the difference in the world. I'm confident, and I believe in what I'm doing. I've got a plan, and I'm just trying to execute it every at-bat and every pitch."

> — **Dansby Swanson,** #1 Overall Draft Pick, *MLB.com*, August 16th, 2017

"It's all information and what you do with it. You're sifting through what works for you and what's not beneficial to your game."

> — **Daniel Murphy,** 3x All-Star and 2x Silver Slugger Award Winner, *The Washington Post*, June 1st 2017

"You got to make adjustments, get to know the pitchers and see what they try to do with you. The hardest part of the game is staying consistent with your plan when you go out there and play the game..."

> — **Didi Gregorious,** *MLB Shortstop, Yahoo Sports*, July 14th, 2017

Key Principles
1. You can't control the result, but you can prepare for it.
2. Nothing changes, if nothing changes.
3. Be curious and willing to risk failure.

Stay Positive!

How many of you take private lesson, after private lesson, hoping to learn the latest hitting approach or pitching mentality? And how many of you watch countless YouTube videos of the pros, looking to pick up tips, and mimic what they do? Most players probably answered "yes" to these questions. But if you could improve your game by simply asking yourself a few questions, would you sign up for that?

5x Gold Glove Award winner and 3x Silver Slugger Award winner, Nolan Arenado, said, "I watch film on some of the best guys like Machado or Beltre to see what they do well, but I always try to stay unique to me, and stay with what I do best." Baseball players need to remain aware of the value of identifying their own strengths and ensuring that those strengths remain the backbone of their game. However, they must always keep an open mind to embrace change and push the limits of their game. With that goal in mind, I have provided seven questions below that will help you to emphasize the positives of your game, while highlighting areas of improvement that require tweaks, change, and even failure, which ultimately aids future success and development.

By identifying these areas, you can use them as the foundation on which to build a solid improvement plan. Additionally, by starting with a positive scenario, you are more likely to make worthwhile changes, and it becomes easier to identify what areas of the game require trial and error. Positivity breeds an attitude that reflects curiosity to explore failure as a way to learn and develop. World Series Champion, Kyle Hendricks, said, "The game is always changing. You can't stay steadfast in what you're doing. You have to look at the other side of it."

Ask yourself:

1. What am I doing in my game that is working?

2. What is behind my overall success?

3. If I could imagine the ideal game—a situation for which I would strive—what would it look like, what would it feel like?

4. What is the difference between where my game is and where I want it to be?

5. What steps do I need to take to address these issues?

6. What resources are available to help me take positive action?

7. When can I start taking action?

Stay Positive!

WORKOUT

1. **What am I doing in my game that is working?** _____
   _____
   _____

2. **What is behind my overall success?** _____
   _____
   _____

3. **If I could imagine an ideal swing, pitch, or situation—what would it look like?**
   _____
   _____
   _____

4. **What is the difference between where my game is and where I want it to be?** ___
   _____
   _____

5. **What steps do I need to take to address these issues?** _____
   _____
   _____

6. **What resources are available to help me take positive action?** _____
   _____
   _____

7. **When can I start taking action?** _____
   _____

2018 National Champions

The process

The outcome
(it was Last out)

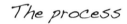

The celebration

BASEBALL
INSIDE THE ZONE

Section 3
IN-GAME WORKOUTS

Workout 17: Between-Pitch Rituals: *Don't Leave Home Without Them!*............................109

Workout 18: Tense, Nervous… Can't Relax? *Five Ways to Manage Pressure*.....................115

Workout 19: Tension, Tears, and Twitches: *The Secret to Managing Stress*........................123

Workout 20: I'm So Tight… *How Can I Loosen Up!?*..123

Workout 21: I SUCK! *How to Tame Negative Self-Talk*...129

Workout 22: You Cannot Be Serious! *Seven Tools to Help You Regain Your Focus*..............135

Workout 23: Bottom of the Ninth. Relax! But How? *Five Steps to Closing Out a Game*.....141

Workout 24: What Do I Do Between Innings? *Keeping Your Focus in the Dugout*.............147

Workout 25: Competing in the Trenchs: *One Part Skill, Three Parts Will*...........................151

Workout 26: Riding the Waves: *Using Momentum to Win*..157

Workout 27: Get Outta Your Mind: *It's the Only Way to Compete!*..................................163

Game Workouts

The Perfect Game

*Three canvas bases
Perfectly Placed.
Home plate and the mound
Perfectly spaced.*

*The chaulk laid down
In a perfect line.
The infield dirt
Raked perfectly fine.*

*Then the teams take the field
And we're reminded again
It's a perfect game
Played by imperfect men.*

By Kevin Coulter.

Workout 17
Mental Point

Rituals help us stay calm, centered, and composed. Having rituals in place between pitches can bring our focus on what we need to do to prepare for the next pitch.

Between-Pitch Rituals:
Don't Leave Home Without Them!

What the Pros Are Saying

"When you have the routine, it helps funnel all that energy and all those thoughts. Everybody's routine and style comes down to their personality, their upbringing, their experience level, and who've they been around…"
— **CJ Wilson,** 2x All-Star, *ESPN.com*, September 6th, 2011

"I try and keep things the same. I have a lot of confidence in my routine…it helps me be relaxed more and be the most relaxed I can be."
— **Jose Quintana,** All-Star Pitcher, *NBC Sports Chicago*, November 2nd, 2017

"I think it just helps with consistency. I think that's the most important thing. If I am able to do the same things leading up to my start day, and if I stink or I don't pitch well, then at least I know I did everything possible to be ready and there's no excuse. I just didn't pitch well."
— **Clayton Kershaw,** 2x Cy Young Award Winner and MVP Award Winner, *ESPN. com*, March 16th, 2014

Key Principles
1. Rituals are the backbone of calmness and comfort.
2. Rituals are a reset button after each pitch to help bring your focus back to what you can control, in the present moment.
3. Rituals should be personal and meaningful to the athlete.

Between-Pitch Rituals

In baseball, and in life, athletes are required to perform under pressure. It's part of the game. Think back to a time you experienced a high-pressure moment in a game. How did you manage it? Picture this, your team is down 3-0, and on the verge of being eliminated from the playoffs. Your team has experienced a long drought. You step back into the box, during a 2-1 count in extra innings, with a man on first, and the chance to win the game

In 2004, just before stepping back into the batter's box, David Ortiz famously put his bat under his right arm, spit in his batting gloves, and clapped them together while staring at the pitcher, just as he routinely does after each and every pitch. On the very next pitch, he delivered a walk-off homerun over the right field wall, as the Red Sox climbed back into the series. With the pressure of a chance to play for the World Series and, end "the curse of the Bambino", his ritual in-between pitches remained consistent.

Whether it's October baseball, a mid-week game, or even a backyard whiffle-ball game, we are always approaching the next challenge and the pressure that goes along with it. When will the next situation occur? And how will you handle it? More importantly, what's your ritual for staying calm and present? More often than not, high-pressure situations can make us feel tense and anxious. They sometimes lead us to second guess our approach and game plan. They take our focus away from the moment, and we begin to run through the various possible outcomes of the situation. However, what if there was a mental-edge tool that we could use to prepare for the situation, and keep us calm yet focused on the task at hand?

Turns out there is, and it's called a ritual. Rituals are pre-programmed processes that can take a ballplayer's mind off of focusing on the result of the situation, by slowing down his internal clock. When a player feels he can no longer contain or manage his emotions during a situation, rituals are used to bring back a sense of comfort, confidence, and most importantly a sense of control.

The ritual that I teach has four stages: The first is the **acknowledgement stage**. Simply make yourself aware of what has happened on the previous pitch. A batter may have chased a ball in the dirt, or a pitcher may have spiked his curveball. However, once you are aware of your current situation, you can then facilitate change and make adjustments. The second stage is your **centering stage**. Step out of the box, or off the rubber, and let go of the previous pitch by bringing your attention to your breathing. The purpose here is to bring your focus to the present moment and balance your internal status with a comfortable breathing tempo. Through your breath, you can focus your mind on an aspect of the game that you control.

The third stage is **strategy**. Decide what the necessary adjustments are, and the best approach to take on the next pitch. Finally, the last stage is the **physical ritual**. The purpose here is to gain control with a familiar action, and subsequently establish your rhythm and timing.

3x All-Star, 3x Gold Glove winner, and Silver Slugger Award winner, Evan Longoria, said, "When the pressure is on, the game becomes more of a mental grind, and that's when we need something to fall back on." Use your own, personal ritual, to reset, and stay on track or when you feel that you have lost control of the situation. By creating a ritual and implementing it in your preparation between pitches, you bolster your physical and emotional preparedness, establishing control and comfort in even the most pressure-packed situations.

Which pitch will you throw?

Between-Pitch Rituals

WORKOUT

Name a player whose ritual you like:

_____

Describe what their ritual looks like:

_____

_____

_____

How do you think it's helpful to them?

_____

_____

_____

How could a ritual be helpful to you?

_____

_____

_____

_____

_____

_____

_____

Create Your Own Unique Between-Pitch Ritual

4 Step Between-Pitch Ritual	What does it mean?	What is the purpose?
1. Acknowledgement Step... ➡	Be aware of what happened ➡	To facilitate change

What do you notice when you acknowledge the previous pitch without judgement?

_____

_____

_____

2. Centering Step ➡	Bring your attention to your breathing ➡	To be grounded in the present moment

What can you do to center yourself (hint: breathing)? What other things could you do?

_____

_____

_____

3. Strategy/Planning Step ➡	Decide what your best options are ➡	To have a plan going into the next pitch/ at bat

What might be an example of a strategy if you are at bat? Or pitching?

_____

_____

_____

4. Physical Ritual Step ➡	Get comfortable with a familiar action ➡	To establish your rhythm

What does your physical ritual look like before an at bat? Or pitch?

_____

_____

_____

Workout 18
Mental Point

We are all born in the present and have the ability to stay in it and play in it.

Tense, Nervous... Can't Relax?
Five Ways to Manage Pressure

<u>What the Pros Are Saying</u>

"There's definitely a different adrenaline when the crowd is into it in a big spot. Channel it into concentration. I've got to mentally bear down in my approach and make sure I get the pitch that I want."
> — **Matt Holiday,** 7x All-Star and 3x Silver Slugger Award Winner, *ESPN.com*, January 10th, 2015

"There are certain things in life we love and we have the chance to pursue, but a lot of the time fear of the unknown, fear of failure gets in the way."
> — **Tim Tebow**, Heisman Trophy Winner and Minor League Player, *ESPN.com*, March 1st, 2017

"Pressure is a moment. Knowing that you're in the playoffs, that's pressure. But knowing that it's where you want to be is what helps."
> — **Mariano Rivera,** 13x All-Star, 5x World Series Champion, and World Series MVP, *cbssports.com* October 29th, 2017

<u>Key Principles</u>
1. Everyone feels fear. It's how you respond to it that counts.
2. Pressure isn't bad, it's a challenge.
3. If you feel pressure, it's because you care.

Tense, Nervous... Can't Relax?

How many times have you heard that the secret to playing your best is being in the present? Have you ever experienced that 'zone'-like time? Conversely, how many times have you experienced being *outside* of the zone, where your thoughts were focused on the previous inning, or hypothetical situations that you may find yourself in later in the game? We all have. You may be walking to the batter's box while still thinking about how you popped up twice in your previous at-bats. Maybe your mind keeps returning to borderline pitches that the ump did not give you a couple innings ago. Why is this? It's actually pretty easy to understand. If you're playing in the past or the future, you have one eye on something you can't control, and the other on the next pitch. Certainly, this is no recipe for success! Your attention is divided.

Here is the good news! The ability to play in the present is something that can be learned and developed. However, it does take discipline, awareness, and the desire to let go of counter-productive thoughts, such as, those you might experience after a strikeout looking or walking the bases loaded. Interestingly, sometimes change is more frightening to a player than continuing to spiral out of control. How often have you witnessed a player with that "deer in the headlights" look, continually being out in front of an off-speed pitch, and refusing to make any type of adjustment? Hence the saying, "it may feel good to swim with an anchor, but the weight of it is going to constantly drag you down." Maybe your swing feels good, and your hands seem fast through the zone, but if your attention is divided on how your swing felt on the previous pitch, you are unable to make the proper adjustments for the next pitch.

It is helpful for a player to use pressure-release practices (PRP) in tight situations when things seem to be going south, or getting out of control, and the game seems to speed up. 2x Silver Slugger Award winner, Jay Bruce, said, "In higher pressure situations your heart starts racing a little bit, your adrenaline gets going a little more. People who are able to slow the game down the most probably are more apt to be more successful in that situation." These PRPs are designed to take your mind off the situation that you're anxious about and refocus your attention on the present. In this refocused state, you can determine where you need to be on the next pitch, instead of over-thinking and analyzing mechanical changes, and approaches in the past or in the future.

The following are five PRPs. You will notice they are called *practices*, not strategies or techniques. This is because they are meant to be practiced both on and off the field. By practicing them, they will become familiar to you and will enable you to access a sense of calmness in a quicker, and deeper fashion. More importantly, with practice comes a greater sense of confidence. Rookie of the Year candidate, Rhys Hoskins, said, "The more reps I get, the more comfortable I feel." Just like every aspect of the game of baseball, the best way to build confidence and comfort is through repetition.

1. Routines: Routines can be very effective for athletes. They are comfortable and consistent, and provide the player a sense of control, confidence, and familiarity. Baseball players develop routines as a part of their preparation because it gives them confidence in their ability to remain focused on the task at hand. This might include a familiar meal routine, batting practice routine, specific throwing sessions, and some relaxation exercises to help them prepare for the game. 4x All-Star and MVP Award Winner, Justin Morneau, uses his on-deck circle routine to prepare himself to "think without thinking."

2. Breathing: I strongly advocate using your breath as a centering and calming practice. By bringing your attention to your breath and noticing its sound, feel, or rhythm, you will automatically bring yourself to the present moment. Most importantly, your breath is something that is in your control. The simple act of doing this, of even asking yourself, "Am I breathing?" will take your mind away from the conscious thought of pressure, help you release tension, and bring your attention to the present. There are many different breathing techniques from which to choose, and the key is to find one that is unique and comfortable to you. Circle back to Workout 11 for examples of breathing techniques that you can utilize during each game!

3. Anchors: An *anchor* is something to which you can bring your attention to, such as a memory, an inspiration, or a designated place on the field that you directly associate with calmness. Evan Longoria said, "If I feel like I lost control of my emotions during the at-bat, that's when I step out of the box, and I always look at the left field foul pole." The *anchor* brings about positive emotions, helps connect to a feeling that facilitates a sense of calm in the body, and gives the player a quick reset to regain control of themselves, and the moment. However, it must be something that can be consistently used, or found in each ballpark. Longoria says, "I use the top of the left field foul pole because I know there is always going to be a top of the foul pole." Developing and focusing on an *anchor* allows the player to let go, release pressure, and center themselves. Your anchor should be personal to you, and just the thought, or vision, of it can lead to tranquility and clarity.

4. Be curious, not furious: This one may sound funny, but just the act of being curious puts you in the present without any preconceived judgments. Being curious creates a sense of awareness of what is happening around you, without thoughts of the past or future getting in the way. Try this: Be curious about your opponent's game without making judgments. What will happen is that you will begin to see patterns emerge. Maybe a pitcher has certain tendencies in his game plan and sequencing of pitches, or a hitter seems to always be taking the first pitch of his at-bat. You will see your opponent's weaknesses and strengths in a way that would not have been possible before, because now you are choosing not to label them or block your awareness with anger. Next time, instead of being angry, frustrated, or even ecstatic at the result, be curious about what happened. When you are curious, you become more consciously aware of the flow of the game. This allows a player to prepare for each situation, by making proper adjustments throughout a game in a calmer fashion.

5. Read the ball: This is a practice that you can do to help you stay present during each pitch. What I mean by this is to focus on the rotation of the ball and track it as it approaches you. You may not see the writing on the ball, however tracking it will help you stay in the moment. By being aware, you will have less time to plan and preconceive if you should swing, or if you should take the next pitch. Although having less time to plan your next swing may sound like a negative, it's not. You may be surprised by how adept your game can be when utilizing your instincts connected with tracking the ball.

Try these 5 Pressure Release Practices; see which ones work best for you. The theme in all of these practices is that they allow you to move away from the stressful situation and offer a sense of calm in return. Once you have attained the calming effect, you can then bring your attention back to the present situation of the game and be able to adjust with clarity. Remember, these are called *practices* for a reason: practice them every day for a few minutes. Over time they will become a comfortable, familiar, and natural part of your game.

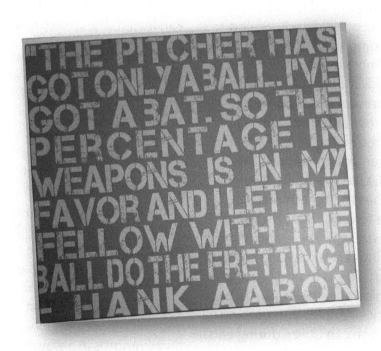

"THE PITCHER HAS GOT ONLY A BALL. I'VE GOT A BAT. SO THE PERCENTAGE IN WEAPONS IS IN MY FAVOR AND I LET THE FELLOW WITH THE BALL DO THE FRETTING." - HANK AARON

Tense, Nervous... Can't Relax?

WORKOUT

In this chapter, I have addressed ideas that can help you slow down, change your focus, and relax during tense situations (routines, breathing, anchors).

Let's briefly explore what can happen in a tense situation. Oftentimes a player will describe their heart speeding up, not feeling certain parts of their body, tension, and a general feeling to speed the game up. On the other hand, players in the zone describe it as relaxed, time slowing down, and playing effortlessly.

Our energy goes up and then naturally comes down like a wave in the ocean, that is unless, fear, anxiety, or a situation threatens us and we spike up (freeze). What is important to understand is that the thought is not the problem; it's when we react to the thought. For example, *I missed that last pitch*, then taking it a step further to mean, *now I'm going to strikeout*.

When fears and anxiety enter your mind, practice not reacting to the fear, but rather just allowing it. Not adding anything to the emotion, just be aware of it. Usually it will go away.

Anchoring Exercise:

Step 1: Think of a time or experience in a game where you faced adversity but overcame it. Describe it.

_____

_____

_____

_____

Step 2: When you think of it, notice how you feel. Describe it.

_____

_____

_____

_____

Step 3: Imagine a situation in the future which may make you feel tight or nervous. Describe it.

_____

_____

_____

_____

Step 4: Now, imagine the time from Step 1 where you turned things around, just noticing that centered, competent feeling...

Step 5: What do you notice?

_____

_____

_____

_____

Now, go back to the future situation that makes you nervous. You may notice that by changing the focus to a feeling of accomplishment (overcoming adversity), the nervousness of the future event may subside and not be as intense as before.

Workout 19
Mental Point

Effectively managing pressure is a counterintuitive process. Rather than ignoring the pressure, it's necessary to accept it. It is what it is.

Tension, Tears, and Twitches:
The Secret to Managing Stress

What the Pros Are Saying

"I'm sticking with the process, If I stick to the process they're (hits) going to fall in."
— **Cody Bellinger,** All –Star and Rookie of the Year Award, *ESPN.com*, October 17th, 2018

"To be a good player, you have to be intense without being tense."
— **Joe Torre,** 9x All-Star, MVP Winner, 2x AL Manager of the Year, and 4x World Series Champion

"There comes a point when the game starts and it's all about competing. If your focus is anywhere else, but to compete you're behind. You should be in the moment."
— **Russell Martin,** 4x All-Star and Gold Glove Winner, *ESPN.com*, March 20th, 2014

Key Principles

1. Every player gets nervous at some point in a game; it's about how you manage it.
2. Just be you, trust your ability.
3. When tense, slow down and focus on your breath.

Tension, Tears, and Twitches

World Series champion Anthony Rizzo said, "There's pressure, no doubt about it, and there's anxiety. It's how you handle it. Do you thrive on it? Do you embrace it? Or do you go into a shell?" How many of you feel pressure making the play in the field to end the game with the tying run on third? Nerves play a key part in any sport, especially in baseball. Nerves can make a player tight; physiologically, the ballplayer will get a surge of adrenaline, his heartbeat pounding like a drum, beads of sweat starting to form on his skin, his breath getting short and shallow as his muscles contract, and his blood pressure increases. All-Star and Gold Glove winner, Brian Dozier, said, "When you get put in certain situations, your heart rate speeds up, but it's good to be nervous. In certain high-pressure situations, you're so intense and you think you're ready to go, but you need to do the opposite: you need to slow the game down."

A common misconception is that the top players don't feel nerves, tension, anxiety, or a fear of failure. NLCS MVP and World Series champion, Matt Holiday, said, "There's an intensity level when you're in a big spot that kicks in, it shouldn't be much different than every other at-bat, but you just can't help it. Naturally, you are much more intense." However, there are mental skills that players utilize to thrive despite the surge of emotions. These players are able to effectively accept these emotions as part of their individual process, and consequently channel them in a manner that allows them to perform in a relaxed state of focused awareness.

You often hear a player say, "If only I wasn't so tight at the plate, I would have been able to hit it!" or, "If I wasn't so nervous and second guessing myself, I would have been able to make that play in the field!" Think about it, how many times have you thrown a baseball? However, you mentally and physically were feeling the pressure of the moment so your throw got away from you. The reality is that you can't separate the mental game from the mechanical and physical adjustments of the game. They work hand in hand, especially in high-pressure situations, and the top pros know it.

Effectively managing pressure is a counter-intuitive process. Rather than ignoring the pressure, it's necessary to accept it. This acceptance neutralizes it or takes the edge off. Most importantly, accepting the situation means you have brought your focus and attention to the present moment. Rejecting, ignoring, or denying the pressure within the situation means the player is distracted by future, or past situations in the game, which further adds to the pressure of the situation. If a player gets up to bat, with the winning run on third and two outs, the situation already is packed with pressure. However, the pressure of the situation becomes even greater if the player is also thinking about their strikeout back in the third inning, and how they need to make up for it. Only upon the acknowledgement that a situation (in this case, the existence of stress) exists in the mind are we able to reduce the tension. 2x All-Star and World Series champion, Miguel Montero, said, "It doesn't matter if you're 0-for-3 or 0-for-4. You might get the biggest at-bat of the game. We need you to be locked in for that. If you keep carrying one at-bat over to the other one, when the big at-bats show up, you're not going to be ready. You're still thinking about the past. You've got to move on."

Media, fans, coaches, and even players often misunderstand nerves, and how to manage them. It's common to hear a statement such as, "champions don't like to admit to nerves." However, even some of games' greatest players admit that they sometimes have difficulty managing their nerves. 5x All-Star and Cy Young Award winner, Zach Greinke, is able to locate his fastball with pinpoint accuracy, but even he admits that sometimes he second guesses his ability because of nervousness. "Every year, I get nervous that it's not working good enough, that it's not going to come fast enough, same thing this year. I think it's going to be ready, but in the back of my mind, I'm always a little nervous that it's not going to be there, and I'm not going to be ready by the time the season starts."

Baseball players on all levels alike are too often discouraged from being honest about their emotions and are consequently compelled to fight an internal battle to deny what they are feeling. Mind you, it's one thing to openly publicize your nervousness to your opponent, but the real trouble comes when an athlete does not privately allow themselves to acknowledge what they are already experiencing. When the athlete fights the emotion, their focus stays on the emotional state (inducing concern or panic over what they are suppressing), rather than accepting it for what it is, and making the choice to move on. Resisting an emotion's existence only makes it stronger.

In conclusion, the machine-like mentality that many people have regarding nerves is misdirected. In fact, it pushes athletes farther from peak performance because they are scared to be themselves, and to fully acknowledge their own mental and emotional experience. Baseball players instinctively understand a key mental edge secret—that it's okay to have nerves. In fact, accepting the experience of acknowledging tension is the first step towards releasing it. World Series Champion winning Manager, Joe Maddon, said, "Once you've done it before, you're not as intimidated by the moment." Think of your emotions the same way, each mental and emotional experience is an opportunity to learn how to channel, harness, and tame your emotions in a manner that benefits you on the field.

Tension, Tears, and Twitches

WORKOUT

The Secret to Managing Stress

"There are two ways to channel nervousness. You can channel into fear or you can channel it into excitement."

— Mark Grace, World Series champion and 4x Gold Glove winner, *ESPN.com*. January 10th, 2015

When was a time you were feeling stressed or nervous in the field, at the plate, or on the mound?

_____

Does this happen often?

_____

What did you do?

_____

_____

What are some things you could do to help release the tension and re-focus? Hint: Refer to the previous chapter for more pressure-release practices; i.e. breathing.

1. _____

2. _____

3. _____

4. _____

5. _____

How could this help you?

_____

_____

_____

Anyone can give
up, it's the
easiest thing in
the world to do.
But to hold it
together when
everyone else
would understand
if you fell
apart, that's
true strength.
~ Anonymous

Workout 20
Mental Point

Your thoughts are not truths and your feelings are not fatal.

Workout 20

I'm So Tight...
How Can I Loosen Up!?

What the Pros Are Saying

"It's all about getting my mind right…that's my number 1 priority. I have my game plan…But you have to be in the present. The here and now. Not in the future. Not in the past."
— **J.D. Martinez,** 2x All-Star and Silver Slugger Award Winner, *WEEI Sports Radio Network*, March 26th, 2018

"Be where your feet are. If your feet are in Fresno, California, that's where your head needs to be. You don't need to be thinking about anything besides the next pitch they're going to throw you."
— **Alex Bregman,** All-Star and World Series Champion, *MLB.com*, April 10th, 2016

"I'm sticking with the process, If I stick to the process they're (hits) going to fall in. "
— **Cody Bellinger,** 2017 All Star and N.L Rookie of the year, *ESPN.com*, October 17th, 2018

Key Principles
1. Turn towards your nerves, not away.
2. Be in the here. Be in the now.
3. Your feet are always where you need to be.

I'm So Tight...

When I first wrote *Baseball Inside the Zone: Mental Training Workouts for Champions*, the number one question players brought to me was, "Omg, I'm Nervous…what do I do?" (see chapter 10). However, there is another question baseball players experience and grapple with that is equally important. These players will say, "I was so tight, when I was swinging the bat it felt like it was a hundred pounds!!" or "I'm so tight, why? My arm feels so slow, I am not going to be able to throw with any velocity behind it!" and "How can I loosen up?"

When a player is noticing tightness, it is most often about anxiety, nervousness, or fear. The description "tight" usually means the player is experiencing one or all of these: shortness of breath, body tingling, lack of energy, clammy skin, overall impatience, and the game seems to speed up.

So, what's a player to do? How do we get back to a more relaxed place, so the game feels effortless, more like practice?

Here are 5 ways a player can loosen up:

1. Stop Fighting:

Rather than fighting your thoughts and feelings and trying to get rid of them, try turning *towards* them and accepting how you feel right now. Simple acceptance eliminates the struggle and allows you the freedom to make adjustments, and find your rhythm and timing. You can "talk" to the feeling and say, "I'm noticing something inside of me is tight." Then, say, "I'm going to say hello to it because it's clearly worried." Then just notice what happens.

This strategy helps you see that your thoughts are not you, nor is the tightness. Rather it's something you are aware of and notice. Thoughts are not truths, and your feelings are not fatal. Think of them like a movie, which you are watching. No need to fuse together with them and allow them to hijack the moment of a pitch or at bat.

2. Shift the Focus:

Most likely the nerves and anxiety is a result of focusing on something you cannot control. Maybe you are trying to control the outcome? What the coach thinks? Or how you "think" you should be playing? All of these things are beyond your control. Shift your focus to something you can control. For example, take 4x All-Star and 2x Gold Glove winner, Manny Machado of the Dodgers. In the 7th game of the National League Divisional Finals he thought the pitcher was "fast pitching" and noticed the infield was back. Uncharacteristically, he laid down a bunt to get on base and began a key 3 run rally. Clearly, he shifted his focus on ways to use his strengths and let go of what he could not control. In his case, it was his speed and feel at the plate. At all times, it's important to break the game into smaller pieces, focusing on one pitch at a time.

3. Shake It Off:

Notice where you are feeling the tightness in your body, if it is in your arm, shake the arm; if it is in your shoulders; shake your shoulders; your legs? Shake them! Shaking can help the body to release tension and feel connected.

You might even ask yourself: "How would I feel if I was loose and relaxed?" Or you can ask this question about a swing. Ask, how would it feel to cut it loose at the plate? Rather than answering this, allow your body to feel and release it. Right now, ask yourself: "How would my jaw feel if it was loose?" If you are like most people, you will realize you have been clenching or holding your jaw tight. Just the awareness will prompt you to let go and release.

4. Breathe:

Bringing your attention to your breath is a secret of so many pros. This allows the player to bring oxygen into the body to replenish and reset. A little-known fact is that by inhaling, you are activating the sympathetic nervous system that provides you with energy. Exhaling activates the parasympathetic nervous system, allowing for calm and relaxation. Breathing in and out serves to ground, balance, and help loosen you up, so you can get out of your mind. It also helps to shift the focus away from the outcome and tightness. Between pitches, in the on-deck circle, or before you step back onto the rubber, bring your attention to your breath and breathe in and out a few times. You won't be sorry.

5. Grounding:

Shift your attention to your feet. Whether you're in the field or in the dugout, notice both of your feet touching the ground. If you are bouncing on your toes or just feeling the balls of your feet, notice the spikes of your cleats making contact with the ground. By doing this, you will become aware that you are stable, balanced, and centered. Being centered will help the nervous system settle.

These five centering tips can be used separately or can be combined into a between-pitch or before game ritual. Be creative. It's important to remember to be present while doing any of these tips. The object, for example, is not to do the breath exercise so you can loosen up. This conditional type thinking will only make you tighter. The idea is to breathe, and to "be the breath." Be present to the breath or shaking or noticing your feet and spikes contacting the ground. By doing this, you have a better chance of settling down. If by chance you don't settle in, don't get upset that you don't feel how you want. Stick to this process, the real game is creating the discipline to be present to the little things. Soon this will translate to bigger things. Joe Maddon once said, "If you take care of the seconds, the minutes, and the hours, the days will take care of themselves." This will allow you the best chance to play the next pitch, out, and game from a centered place.

I'm So Tight...

WORKOUT

"That stress is there for your own benefit. And it is not stress. It is an opportunity."

— Ben Zobrist, 3x All-Star and 2x World Series Champion,
SportingNews.com, April 30th, 2018

What was a time you felt tight?

_____

_____

What did you experience?

_____

_____

_____

_____

Where in your body did you feel the tightness?

_____

How did this affect your performance?

_____

_____

_____

_____

From the workout, list three things you can do next time to shift your focus.

1. _____

2. _____

3. _____

Workout 21
Mental Point

The best players in the world have doubts, fears, and nerves in different situations throughout the game. It happens to everyone. The question becomes: how will you respond and play through it? Will you allow the fear of making a mistake dictate the way you approach the game?

I SUCK!
How to Tame Negative Self-Talk

What the Pros Are Saying

"Expect something good to happen. Every time you step up there expect something good …If it doesn't happen, it doesn't matter. There's always the next at-bat and tomorrow's another day"

— **David Peralta,** MLB Outfielder, Arizona Diamondbacks, *AZ Central*, April 23rd, 2018.

"When it's my turn to hit, the quietest place on earth is home plate."

— **Ted Williams,** Hall of Fame Outfielder, *ESPN.com*, May 2nd, 2013

"Whatever I hit last series is gone. It doesn't count for this series. So, if someone asks me. 'what is your batting average right now?' I would say 'it's zero', I haven't got a hit in the next series."

— **Jose Altuve,** World Series Champion, MVP Winner, and 6x All-Star, *ESPN.com*, October 11th, 2017

Key Principles

1. Look at what is happening, not what has happened.
2. Negative self-talk comes from a part of you that is afraid. Allow it and move on.
3. The secret to managing self-talk is to simply notice it, but not get caught up in it.

I SUCK!

If we are honest with ourselves, all players experience negative thoughts from time to time. It starts with that devilish, little voice in our head, which raises doubts, fears, and questions about our ability to perform. The little voice usually comes during the pressure-packed situations in a game. It's that voice that says, "you don't stand a chance against this pitcher's heater" or "your stuff is not good enough to get this guy out." It's that cynical, little voice that whispers, "if you strikeout again, coach is probably going to pinch hit for you next time you're up," or, "I hope the error I made didn't ruin my pitcher's tempo, and he's not mad at me." Negative thoughts precede negative self-talk. Without the proper awareness, they can bring down even the most competitive player.

When a player chooses to listen to his negative thoughts and begins self-talk, that's when the downward spiral usually begins. It often looks something like this: a player boots a routine ground ball, and in their head the little voice of doubt enters and begins chiming in with negative thoughts. Simultaneously, their body starts to get tight, and the game begins to speed up. Instead of moving to the next play and the next pitch, taking a deep breath, and re-centering, the verbal and negative self-talk begins. The player continues to harp on the previous mistake, how it has affected the game, or how it will affect the game in the later innings.

What's important to understand is that we have a choice regarding how to react or respond to our negative thoughts. When we react to our negative thoughts with defensiveness and deny their existence, the voice gets louder and louder. Picture yourself inside a packed stadium. There is a fan who is constantly heckling you. The only voice you can hear is the voice of the fan trying to bring you down. There is a saying— "What you resist, persists." In other words, by ignoring this voice or feeling, it is only going to become louder, until it is the only thing being heard. It's also important to understand that just because you conjured up this negative thought doesn't mean that your thought is the truth. For example, have you ever been down in the count and said to yourself: "this at-bat is over; I don't stand a chance against his breaking ball," only to foul off a couple tough pitches before working the count back to your favor, and getting a base hit? This is because you accepted this thought, not as true or false, or as a validation of anything, but just non-judgmentally.

So, what can a player do when they are bombarded with negative self-thoughts, especially in the thick of a late inning situation? Here are six practices you can use when negative self-thoughts start creeping into your head—before negative self-talk begins to affect your ability to perform on the diamond.

1. Be aware, and watch it dissolve away: The problem is not the self-thoughts— those are normal. Don't resist it or fight with it. Instead, simply understand that it's a by-product of being in a high-pressure situation. With awareness of self-thoughts, take a step back, bring your attention to your breath, and visualize the self-thoughts being released with your exhalation.

2. Welcome and normalize: Tip your cap in acknowledgment to your self-thoughts— by acknowledging them, you normalize them. You can actually say to these self-thoughts, "Hey, thanks for sharing your concerns, but I'm in the middle of a game. Go back to the stands."

3. Put a time lid on it: Here, the concept of acceptance comes through once again. If you find yourself muttering "I stink" after missing a pitch, or after a game. Rephrase that by saying, "I missed that pitch, I'll have plenty of other opportunities." Even after a game, many times a player will walk off the field with his confidence being broken because he keeps telling himself, "I suck." While, ideally, the young player would not feel this way to begin with, a realistic and far healthier approach would be, "I had a bad game today. Time to rebound."

4. Reframe the situation: Imagine it's a 1-2 count in the bottom of the 9th, and you're about to deliver the pitch to close out the game. The thought comes up: "Uh oh, I'm so nervous. What if I hang this pitch and he hits it out?" Ask yourself: what's another way of looking at this? How about considering the opportunity to deliver the best off-speed pitch you've ever thrown?

Instead of dwelling on the obstacles associated with our nerves, we can shift attention to the process that entails what we must do— to make you get enough spin on the ball, and to make sure you hit the catchers target located on the outside corner.

5. Change your focus: A great example of turning negative thoughts around, and shifting your focus to something positive and calming, is what All-Star Chad Cordero said: "For me, self-talk was singing to myself on the mound. That is pretty much what helped me relax. I'd usually sing whatever song I heard last. In my head, I always had a tune and that kind of helped me focus, relax, and stay confident."

6. Glove talk: Your glove is a great reason and excuse to take a moment to regroup. Tune into any game and you will always see players talking into their gloves, as pitchers and catchers talk during a mound visit, or middle infielders communicate who's got the bag on steal. However, talking into your glove can be used to release negative thoughts, or to offer yourself words of encouragement, like "I've got this."

In summary, we all have negative self-thoughts. When you sense them escalating to self-talk, you need to regain control of the situation. All players will have doubts, fears, and nerves throughout a game. The question becomes how you will respond, play through it, and avoid the negative spiral downward. When in doubt, go back to the above six practices.

I SUCK!

WORKOUT

The Art of Talking to Yourself!

We all talk to ourselves... you know that little inner judgmental critic that says "you shoulda done this," or "you coulda done that." Sometimes the critic even calls you names! "I'm an idiot" or "I can't believe I did that!"

Can you recall a game when you were highly frustrated?_____

Describe the situation:

_____

_____

_____

With that game in mind, list all the negative things you thought or said aloud. (Be honest!)

1. _____

2. _____

3. _____

4. _____

5. _____

Looking at this list, what does it make you aware of?

_____

_____

How did saying these things affect your confidence and performance?

_____

_____

_____

Would you say these things to your best friend? _____

Why not?

_____

_____

What could you do to bounce back from the mistakes?

1. _____

2. _____

3. _____

How would this be helpful?

_____

_____

_____

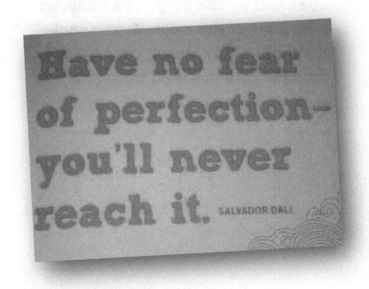

Have no fear of perfection—you'll never reach it. SALVADOR DALI

Workout 22
Mental Point

Recall a time you were on the diamond and lost your focus due to a bad call by the ump, a bad hop, or even a pitch you missed. The real challenge is regaining your focus and bringing yourself back to a place of calmness.

You Cannot Be Serious!
Seven Tools to Help You Regain Your Focus

What the Pros Are Saying

"I think you just try not to get caught up in it….From my standpoint I'm just going to focus on the team and try to just just go about my business as usual. Focus on that and I think the rest of the stuff will take care of itself. Otherwise, it just adds more pressure to the situation"

    — **J.A. Happ,** All-Star Pitcher, *MLB.com*, March 1st, 2018.

"You come to the plate so many times, so many games, so many pitchers and your mind starts wandering. After I lost my concentration, I'd swing at a ball and hit it and make an out and come back to the bench and I'd say, 'Why did I swing at that ball?' It's that concentration is gone."

    — **Stan Musial,** Hall of Fame Outfielder and First Baseman, *Sporting News*, July 11th, 2009.

"My ability to fully focus on what I had to do on a daily basis was what made me the successful player I was. Sure, I had some natural ability, but that only gets you so far. I think I learned how to focus; it wasn't something that I was necessarily born with."

    — **Hank Aaron,** Hall of Fame Outfielder, <u>*Heads-Up Baseball: Playing the Game One Pitch at a Time,*</u> May 11th, 1998

Key Principles

1. Expect the unexpected.
2. Concentrating 100% of the time is not important. Understanding when you lose your concentration and bringing it back to the present is important!
3. The most important pitch is the NEXT pitch.

You Cannot Be Serious!

"**Y**ou **cannot** be serious! That pitch was outside! How can you call that a strike? You can't keep giving this pitcher these calls!" How many times have you seen players who understand the strike zone better than most, like Joey Votto or Mike Trout, who have finished a season leading the league in walks, turn around and say something to the ump after a questionable call?

Certainly, we have all seen professionals lose their focus. However, the question is, how many of you can recall a time you were on the field and lost your focus due to a borderline pitch not going your way, a bad hop in the field—or, even because you missed your pitch. The real challenge is regaining your focus, and bringing yourself back to a place of calm, where you're able to focus on the next pitch without remnants of the past, or distractions about the future.

It is important to understand that paradoxically, you must be aware of having lost your focus in the first place! It sounds simple, even obvious. Only when you recognize the slippery slope of potential self-destruction are you able then to rebound. Think about it, how many times have you lost your composure on questionable calls early in an at-bat, and it had gone on to affect the rest of your at-bat? You start focusing on thoughts like, "now I'm behind in the count, when I should be ahead" or "that pitch just changed the whole dynamic of this at-bat." The slope of these thoughts is much like the action of dominos falling, gaining momentum as they go. With awareness, you can choose to respond to the adverse situation by slowing down and making the conscious choice to take control of your focus on the next pitch. Be aware and proud that it takes courage to change your focus from where you were and reach a place of composure. In tough situations, try using the following tools to regain your focus or stay on track:

1. Rituals. The power of rituals lies in the fact that they are predictable actions that a player can always rely on to feel more comfortable during an unpredictable situation. For this reason, rituals will help to bring you back to a place of calm. You can refer to Workout 17, for between pitch rituals, to help get you started developing your own set of rituals!

2. Self-coaching. With self-coaching, players ask themselves questions that result in beneficial, physiological responses. For example, there are a number of questions you can ask yourself, such as, "If I were relaxed, what would it feel like?" or, "If I let my instincts take over, what would it feel like?" Inevitably, your body's natural physiological response will be to release tension, become curious, and return to the present moment.

3. Reframing thoughts. Much like self-coaching, reframing your thoughts requires that you assess the immediate situation, and employ alternative techniques to help you stay calm. For example, you may find yourself saying, "Here we go again, this ump keeps squeezing me!" Rather than fighting these thoughts, try reframing them. You can say something like: "Maybe I don't have the inner half now, but now let's concentrate on keeping the hitters off balance by changing speeds," or, "Yeah, this is a pressure-packed moment, but it's the opportunity I've worked hard to put myself in." Remember, it is okay to be nervous. It's even natural; it means you care!

4. Anchors. Before each game, create an anchor: choose something that elicits a sense of calm. It might be a song, a memory linked with relaxation, or maybe it's just an area in the ball park that you directly link with regrouping or resetting. When you feel like you have lost control during the game, focus on recalling the emotions, thoughts, and feelings you associate with that anchor (you can even refer to Workout 18, where Evan Longoria discussed his own use of an anchor). By allowing yourself this mental break, you can mentally return to the game fresh and clear.

5. Cue cards. Before each game, prepare a few pertinent words, phrases, or quotes that may help you relax. Write statements on a card that can fit in your back pocket, on the brim of your hat, on your wrist tape, or anywhere that is easily accessible to you. For example, World Series Champion and 2x All-Star, Dontrelle Willis, used to write "Have Fun," and his mother's name, Joyce, under the brim of his cap, and World Series Champ and Cy Young Award winner, Barry Zito, used to write "FITZ", on the brim of his cap, which stood for, "Fearless In The Zone."

6. Breathing. Bring your attention to your breath—the body and the breath are always in the present moment. By simply noticing your breath's natural rhythm, either the sound or the feel of it, you will bring yourself into the present. Sometimes, noticing your breath can be too or passive for some players, and they become impatient. If this happens to you, be more active, and visualize yourself breathing in relaxation and breathing out stress. Say or think the words as you do this. Another breathing exercise is to inhale to the count of three, and exhale to the count of four. Hitting a fastball is hard enough but imagine how much harder it is when your mind is moving faster than that fastball!

7. Eye-of-the-hurricane focusing. To use eye-of-the-hurricane focusing, bring your attention to an object, and focus on it. This narrowing of your focus will help you eliminate outside distractions. You may want to focus on the bat in your fingertips, or even how the seams of the ball feel in your hand as you grip your pitch. Once you are focused on your object of choice, you can then begin to expand your focus, and take in everything around you. You will find this narrow-to-wide focusing to be very calming, because you are controlling what aspects of the game you are letting into your line of focus.

Regaining your focus is a challenge. Learning to adapt to the ever-changing dynamics on the field is empowering, and a key to playing your best. All of the tools above can help you slow down, relax, regain composure, and let go of adverse situations.

You Cannot Be Serious!

WORKOUT

Tools to Help You Regain Your Focus

The idea behind concentration is not necessarily to focus 100% of the time, but to know when you have lost your focus, and regain it. Try the exercises below for five minutes each.

NO DISTRACTION EXERCISE:

Step #1: With your eyes closed, notice your breath as you inhale and exhale.

Step #2: As you inhale, visualize the number 1; as you exhale, silently **say** the number 1. Repeat this process.

Step #3: If you get distracted or lose focus of the number 1, gently move on to the number 2 and visualize the number 2.

What number did you reach?_____

What did you do when you lost your concentration?

_____

_____

DISTRACTION EXERCISE:

Now, let's incorporate distractions. Turn on the TV, or have a friend try to distract you. Either way, close your eyes and follow the no-distraction protocol. Expect to lose your focus many more times.

What number did you reach?_____

How was this different?

_____

_____

Is it bad that you're losing your focus?

_____

_____

The answer is no: What is important is understanding that you *will* lose your focus. What's key is bringing your focus back to what's important and what you can control at that time. It's impossible to focus 100% of the time. The top pros know how to relax and then focus at key times.

When you lose your focus, what are two things you can do to regain it?

1. _____

2. _____

"ANY TIME YOU HAVE AN OPPORTUNITY TO MAKE A DIFFERENCE IN THIS WORLD AND YOU DONT, THEN YOU ARE WASTING YOUR TIME ON EARTH."
—ROBERTO CLEMENTE—

Workout 23
Mental Point

Losing focus is a natural a part of the game that each player experiences. However, the key is being aware that you lost your focus and making the adjustment to bring yourself back to the present.

Bottom of the Ninth... Relax! But How?
Five Steps to Closing Out a Game

What the Pros Are Saying

"The 27th out is the most crucial because it's the last out of the game. You can't end the game until you get the 27th."

> —**Jeff Banister**, AL Manager of the Year, *WFAA 8 ABC*, May 31st, 2017

"There is nothing like the electricity of the ninth inning in a one-run game. The emotion and elevated heartbeats of all those present turn just another inning into a 'pressure' situation."

> — **Huston Street,** Rookie of the Year and 2x All-Star, *ESPN.com*, June 2nd, 2005

"I think the best thing I try to think about is that once that ball leaves my fingers, I am no longer in control of it. So, I mean it could be a perfectly located, really good breaking ball and the guy hits one off the end of the bat and it falls in. I can't control that. The only thing I can focus on is trying to make a good pitch and then moving on to the next one."

> — **Cody Allen,** MLB Relief Pitcher, *Stack.com*, February 1st, 2017

Key Principles

1. The last 3 outs of a game are the toughest
2. An opponent is most dangerous when he plays as if he has nothing to lose.
3. Closing out games is hard—expect the unexpected!

Bottom of the Ninth... Relax! But How?

It's the bottom of the 9th inning, your team is down by 2 runs, with a man on second base. Your team's clean-up hitter steps in the box and delivers a 2-run homerun to tie the game! Your team begins to feel a wave of momentum, and they feed off the energy from the fans cheering. The next batter hits a triple!!! Your heart starts racing, because it is now your turn to hit, with the opportunity to possibly win the game. As you walk slowly to the plate your focus shifts from the present to the uncontrollable future. You begin to visualize your teammates running out of the dugout, throwing your helmet up in the air, and the feeling of success after you deliver a walk-off base hit up the middle. At the same time, you begin to visualize the repercussions if you are not able to come up in the clutch. You start to think about what it would be like if you were to strikeout or roll over on a pitch for an easy out.

All baseball players have had these thoughts. The question becomes: Which players had allowed their mind to focus on uncontrollable events in the future during late game situations, and as a result of not keeping their focus in the present moment, have gone on to lose a game? While it is true that even the game's best players may lose their focus during critical situations, the truly mentally tough competitors become aware when this happens and are able readjust their focus back to the present moment. In game 6 of the 2002

World Series, The San Francisco Giants relinquished a 5 to 0 lead over the Anaheim Angels in the bottom of the 7th inning. They went on to lose the game 6 to 5, and they would eventually go on to lose game 7, 4 to 1. As the Angels were able to ride the wave of momentum of a big come-back win to capture a World Series title! Do you think the Giants lost focus of the present moment, and started to feel and visualize the win prematurely?

Losing focus is a natural, a part of the game that each player experiences. However, the key is being aware that you lost your focus and making the adjustment to bring yourself back to the present. The problem is, that when it's happening, you may swear that you are concentrating. And you probably are—just on the wrong thing! Focusing on the events of the future immediately removes you from the present moment and takes you to a place where you no longer have control. As your thoughts drift into the future, you lose touch with what you must do to be prepared for the next pitch.

When you lose focus, you usually begin to get tight. Physiologically, the blood flow gets diverted away from your arms and legs, and your breathing becomes labored instead of deep and controlled. Next comes a loss of feel for rhythm and timing at the plate, on the mound, and in the field. All of these physiological responses, combined with future-oriented thinking, cause your game to spiral further out of control. Players begin to feel the game slipping away from them. The pressure and intensity grow with each pitch. Hitting and throwing mechanics become second guessed, as the bat is no longer held loosely in the finger tips, and the seams of the ball are gripped tighter.

So, what can a player do? No doubt this is a difficult situation, but by employing the following five mental-toughness strategies—especially when you find your game spiraling out of control in late inning situations—you can give yourself the opportunity to get back on track and turn things around.

1. Become aware. The first step to combating loss of focus is to become aware that you have indeed lost it. When we talk about 'concentration' in baseball, we are referring to the ability to focus on what you can control on the next pitch. All players lose their focus at times throughout a game; it's inevitable. The truly mentally-tough players don't beat themselves up when it happens, instead, they immediately bring their focus back to what they can control.

2. Re-focus on the present. This is imperative, but how can you do it? First off, know that it takes a lot of courage and discipline to mentally re-focus. However, what's the alternative? A free fall! To re-focus, bring your attention to your breath. Your breath is always present: just listen to it and its rhythm, and how it feels as it enters and leaves your body. Visualize yourself breathing relaxation in, and breathing stress out, slowly slowing the game back down. We are taught that

hitting and pitching is about finding your rhythm and timing. Use your breath as an anchor to find a comfort in your rhythm and timing on the mound, and at the plate. Another present-moment awareness exercise is to breathe in through your nose to the count of three (if possible), and out through your mouth to the count of four. Or, make up your own pattern. When you feel like you lost control, call time and step out of the box, or step off the rubber, and reset yourself. Use these breathing techniques to stay calm, relaxed, and mentally present.

3. Change focus. Inevitably, baseball players tend to lose focus when they think about future situations in a game. They tend to create hypothetical scenarios that might occur, and how they would react, and perform during them. The key here is to recognize that your mind is generating uncontrollable situations and bring your focus back to the pitch that is about to be delivered.

4. Let go of winning and of expectations. Remember, you cannot control whether you win or lose, or whether or not you come through with a walk-off hit—your opponent has a say in that. The more you focus on the outcome, the more physically tense you will become. Just prepare and play each pitch the best you can; if you do this, you will put yourself in the best position to succeed. If you don't win, you will understand that sometimes that's the way the game goes, but you will feel confident in the way you were able to adapt and adjust to each situation throughout the game.

5. Trust your process. Bring your attention to what you have to do to execute in late inning situations. This may include using your anchors to stay relaxed, or maybe asking yourself what it would feel like to put a good swing on the ball. Your body knows; now is the time to trust it. Then maybe ask yourself what it would feel like to play effortlessly. MVP and 2x Silver Slugger Award winner, Josh Donaldson, said, at the plate, "I like to use the term effortless bat-speed. It is not taking all my energy to produce bat speed. I swing effortlessly."

Using the strategies above will help you prepare for the next pitch, the inning, and the game. They will help you play from a calm and relaxed place. Remember in the bottom of the ninth… relax! …Now you know how!

Bottom of the Ninth... Relax! But How?

WORKOUT

Try Softer, Not Harder

One of the biggest mental traps that baseball players fall into is **"trying too hard."** **Fueled by frustration** or making the game too important, trying too hard is usually a game of diminishing returns: The harder you try, the worse you'll do!

This is because **you put pressure on yourself,** rush yourself, and your **muscles tighten up.**

Peak performance always comes from being in a **state of relaxed awareness**, a place of letting go, where the actions happen without much conscious effort or thought.

When you become aware of **yourself trying too hard**, pressing, or rushing... **Shift your focus** of concentration away from the outcome or its importance to the present task at hand.

Remember you want to **relax and try "softer," not harder**.

What does the passage above make you aware of?

_____

_____

_____

How does this apply to your game?

_____

_____

_____

In order to try softer, not harder, what are three things you could do?

1. _____

2. _____

3. _____

Workout 24
Mental Point

Most players view their time in the dugout as time to take a mental break from the game. While this can be helpful, how you prepare while in the dugout waiting for either your next at-bat, or the next time you head into the field, is a crucial aspect of the game that often gets overlooked.

What Do I Do Between Innings?
Keeping Your Focus in the Dugout

What the Pros Are Saying

"You can't deny the fact that you know it's a big situation. You can't deny reality. The heart is racing, there's a heightened sense of focus because of the gravity of the moment. You have to look at those things as good things."

— **Ben Zobrist,** Chicago Cubs, *www.sportingnews.com,* 2018

"For me, all my negative thoughts that I have about, 'How did you miss that pitch? Why did you miss that pitch? You shouldn't have missed that pitch.' I just kind of sit there and kind of crush it up, and once I'm done doing that… I kind of just toss it aside…Start fresh and get back in the box and get back to your positive thoughts."

— **Aaron Judge,** New York Yankees, *ESPN.com,* July 18th, 2017

Key Principles

1. Create a positive internal dialogue.
2. Reset your mind and focus.
3. Just do you.

What Do I Do Between Innings?

In the 2017 World Baseball Classic Team Cuba's Youelqui Cespedes, younger brother of 2x All-Star and Silver Slugger Award winner, Yoenis Cespedes, smacked a RBI single into right field to produce the first run of the game. After eventually coming around to score, the camera scanned the dugout to find Youelqui Cespedes with his arms back, feet kicked up, laughing with his teammates, all while enjoying an ice-cold apple juice box!

Maintaining your focus in the present moment for an entire game is difficult, in fact, it's simply not realistic. Therefore, part of your time spent in the dugout needs to be used to decompress, maybe even to reset.

During the 4th inning of every home game, the Washington Nationals host their infamous Presidents Mascot race. In his debut season with the Nationals, and despite immensely struggling at the plate, All-Star outfielder Jayson Werth decided to release the burden of underperforming by joining in the race! As a matter of fact, the team's entire bullpen decided to join in on the action as well! Jayson Werth and the Nationals bullpen pinned the mascots along the right field wall. With no mascots left to race, Jayson Werth was able to cross the finish line victorious!

The game of baseball is a mental grind. However, even the big leaguers realize that the time spent in-between innings, and in the dugout, is valuable time that

can be used to decompress! It is time that can be used to release energy, and help players settle themselves. I often tell the players that I work with that it is ok to take your time in-between innings, and in the dugout, to step back, let your guard down, and soak in the atmosphere around you.... it is all about bringing your focus back to where it needs to be to perform at your highest level when it counts! However, the next question then becomes, after you settle in, where should you bring your attention to next, to regain your focus on the present moment? The answer to this question is to then to take some time to fill your back pocket!

How many times have you seen a player jog off the field after a half inning of play and head right to the bench to restock their back pocket with either chewing gum, sunflower seeds, or even their batting glove? Players have a lot of time in the dugout and their minds can wander. Certainly, allowing yourself to settle after a big play or inning in the field is an absolutely a necessity, but then it becomes about coming back to center.

Players who are due up that inning may focus on what they need to do succeed in their next at bat. For example, they may focus on their approach based on the pitcher, "look away, and adjust to the inside pitch." Or maybe they start to get their timing based on how the pitcher warms up. Pitchers often will sit themselves in isolation and focus on what part of the lineup is due up in the next half inning, and what type of game plan they are going to execute. However, what if you're not due up, and you're not on the mound, where should you bring your attention and focus to?

What if there was a way to mentally re-fuel yourself and use this time spent in the dugout to metaphorically fill your back-pocket, and not just with seeds, gum, or your batting gloves? But, fill your back-pocket with successful moments you have experienced as a player. For example, it can be a time where you felt you put your most effortless and best swing on a pitch either in a game or in practice. Or as a pitcher, a time you were clicking on all cylinders and you were hitting all of your spots.

By filling your back-pocket with positive memories you are creating an internal anchor that helps keep you calm, confident, and mentally sharp. Additionally, it will keep your mind from focusing on past plays in the field or at the plate, or even from drifting to the future. Use your time in the dugout to filling your back-pocket with experiences that give you confidence as a player.

Think about this, it's the bottom of the ninth, with 2 outs, the winning run on third, and a playoff-birth on the line. You're 0-for-3 at the plate, and you have felt completely uncomfortable all day standing in the box. You're nervous, and your mind is racing back and forth between your previous at bats and what it will feel like if you can't come through with a clutch hit.

Call time, step out of the box, bring your attention to your breath and reach into your back- pocket. Pull out that "moment" which you brought up in the dugout. Allow yourself to feel the sensations as you remember it, as a reminder that you have had many great at-bats during critical situations, and that your previous at bats do not have to dictate your swing on the next pitch.

Maybe you pull out a time you know you weren't overthinking at the plate, and you turned perfectly on an inside pitch and drove it into the gap. That play gives you a sense of confidence and resets your mind on a time you were present, rather than overthinking about the pressure of the situation.

If you know where you are
You will know what you need
Come home: be still
Listen to the echo of your silence
R. Polishook

What Do I Do Between Innings?

WORKOUT

Filling Your Back-Pocket

"I'm doing something that's going to help me when I'm out there, not just vegging on the bench….It takes a lot of work to get those positive thoughts in your head, the ones you want there, as opposed to the ones that creep in there."

— **Roy Halladay,** Philadelphia Phillies, *www.thestar.com*, March 12, 2007

Take a few minutes to fill your back-pocket.

Below write out 5 positive experiences that stick out in your mind, where you felt you were performing with a clear and calm mind. They should be not be mechanical things, but simply at bats, plays in the field, or times on the mound which help you relax. They can also serve as a reminder of your ability to perform at the highest level!

1. _____

2. _____

3. _____

4. _____

5. _____

The time you spend in the dugout is valuable and should be utilized wisely. The experiences you fill your back-pocket with can help you remain calm, centered, and mentally focused throughout the game. The experiences can help you reframe negative thinking to into positive optimism!

Workout 25
Mental Point

**Competing is adapting and
adjusting to what is happening.**

Competing in the Trenchs:
One Part Skill, Three Parts Will

What the Pros Are Saying

"We had some goals that we set out to accomplish. Developing a culture of competition, of effort every single day, that allows players to reach their abilities and reach their full potential."

> — **Craig Counsell,** 2x World Series Champion, *USA Today Network*, October 4th, 2016

"I can't look at the big picture of the season… my goal is to go out there and compete outing after outing and get the job done."

> — **Craig Kimbrel,** Rookie of the Year Award Winner and 7x All-Star, *SBnation.com*, January 30th, 2013

"We go out and compete every night to the best of our ability, and not look beyond the moment….to be competitive means to go out there and focus, be mentally tough, and to earn everything on the field."

> — **Torey Lovullo,** World Series Champion and NL Manager of the Year, *ArizonaSports.com*, November 7th, 2016

Key Principles
1. Play proud.
2. Your opponent is your partner, not the enemy.
3. Play within yourself, not without!

Competing in the Trenchs

It's the dog days of summer. It's the stretch of the season between July and August, where the sun is beating down with no cloud cover in sight. The air is thick and humid. The grass and dirt are dry, filled with divots and bad hops! It's that time of the season… Your spikes are worn down so much that you begin to feel the burning of the rubber on the soles of your shoes. Your legs are so tired that simply getting into a pre-pitch ready position is a strenuous task. You take your sunglasses off the top of your hat and put them on, but it's still too bright, so you use your glove to shield the sun as well. It has been a long game, and you've been on the field for hours… However, now it's extra innings, and the score is tied 1 to 1. It has been a pitcher's duel, as runs have been hard to come by. You remember what your coach said: *"Finding a way to win is three-parts will and one-part skill."* At this point, you know it's all about willing yourself to make the best adjustments to compete.

You reflect back and remember the hours of training you put in running, lifting weights, bullpen sessions, taking ground balls, and hitting off the tee, all to condition yourself for these moments. You also think of all the mental training you have practiced. Exhaustion is setting in. Like a pitcher with a rising pitch count, struggling to find the zone, you wonder how much you have left in the tank. It's decision time. Either you push through and make adjustments to compete, or you give in and fold. Another thought crosses your mind... why are you doing this in the first place? You have made it your motto to compete to the fullest each and every pitch. *You remind yourself to bring your attention to your breath—it's so simple and always seems to calm you and bring your focus back to the present moment.*

This game has been a pitching and defensive battle. You still can't believe how well the other team's pitcher is mixing speeds and commanding each pitch. Okay, that's well beyond your control now. It's late in the game, and it seems like the next run will be the difference maker. With each pitch, the magnitude and importance of it grows. Once again, your coach says, *"The key to ideal competing is adapting and adjusting to what is currently happening."*

You know changing your approach is essential to get on base. Typically, you like to look for fastball in, something you can turn on. However, this pitcher has been painting the outer black all game. You decide to adopt an opposite field approach, and since he has been giving every hitter a steady dose of off-speed, you decide to sit on his curveball. If you can pick up the spin on his hand, and see the pitch deep, you can shoot it the other way for a hit. Usually, sitting on a pitch on the inner half is where you feel the most comfortable. However, being on the field for so long baking in the sun, and involved in such a pitcher duel, this situation is not usual! As your coach always says, *"The ability to be aware of what is going on each pitch and the willingness to adopt a new approach when necessary are what separate the top 1% of competitors from the other 99%."*

The score is still tied in extra innings, and you're due up third. The lead-off batter doubles, and the next guy bunts him over. It's time to change your approach once again. You are aware that a simple fly ball will get the job done. Now you are looking for a pitch in a location that you can either drive or get in the air. You focus on getting your rhythm and timing. You keep fouling off pitches until you get the pitch in the location that you can get the job done. Your ego wants you to be a hero, to hit a go-ahead homer. But you have pushed that to the side. You do not worry about the other at-bats you have had earlier in the game. You buy into the approach and strategy, and continue to battle until you get a pitch in the location you are looking.

The pitcher looks rattled. He is upset and frustrated because you have fouled off some of his best pitches, and he seems anxious due to the pressure of the situation. You are not fazed by his antics and you remain focused on the job at hand. You don't allow his emotions to impact your

own. *In order to compete at your best, in any situation, you have to respect the game and your opponent. This mindset keeps me in a focused, centered place.*

It's a 2- 2 count. The pitcher starts his delivery, and as soon as the ball breaks his glove and his comes arm up behind his ear, you manage to pick up the grip of the ball. It's a fastball! As the ball leaves his hand you realize that the pitch is going to be up in the zone. You jump all over it and drive the ball into the gap. You got the job done! You just won in extra innings.

This win was not easy; it ultimately wasn't about skill, but about making adjustments to best compete in the moment. You had to adapt and adopt different approaches as the situation changed. You had to battle to bring your focus on what you could control, and let go of what you could not. You had to battle without expectations, be willing to put your ego aside, and through it all you had to zone in to what was necessary to accomplish for each pitch and situation. These are the skills necessary to compete at your highest level. These are the tools used in mastering the science of competeology (See Workout #4).

Competing in the Trenchs

WORKOUT

Pre-Game Intangibles Scale

"Competing is not trying hard. Everybody tries hard in the big leagues; I never met a big leaguer who didn't try hard. Competing is making adjustments throughout the game to try and figure out how to beat the guy on the mound, or if you're on the mound, figuring out how to beat the guy in the batter's box. That's competing."

— **Scott Servais,** Former MLB Manager

This exercise will help you rate, become aware, and better understand key intangible factors when playing. Rate yourself (scale: 0 = not at all; 10 = very much).

Opponent:_____

Game/Series/Tournament:_____

Date:_____

	Myself	Opponent
Confidence:		
Momentum coming into the game		
Experience factor		
Physical readiness		
Mental readiness		
Hunger factor		
Concentration:		
Ability to focus on controllables		
Ability to manage uncomfortable situations		
Ability to make opponent uncomfortable		
Ability to stay emotionally balanced, and re-focus		
Awareness		
Compete:		
Ability to stay the course (resilience, tenacity)		
Ability to bounce back from adversity/obstacles/setbacks (perseverance)		

Baseball Inside the Zone™

Ability to adapt/adjust, switch approaches (flexibility)		
Ability to make high-percentage choices		
Ability to play within self, take what opponent is giving you (patience)		

What does analyzing the Intangibles Scale make you aware of?

_____

_____

_____

What are you aware of in relation to your opponent?

_____

_____

_____

From the above, what are three things that would help you as you prepare for the match?

1. _____

2. _____

3. _____

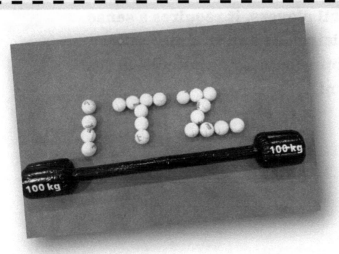

How strong is your mental game?
Get iTZ! (Inside the Zone)

Workout 26
Mental Point

Only by challenging yourself to catch the "big wave" and testing one's limits will true potential be uncovered; for surfers and baseball players, it requires a sense of anticipation and timing, while remaining calm and centered in the moment.

Riding the Waves:
Using Momentum to Win

What the Pros Are Saying

"Momentum is as good as the next game's starting pitcher."

> — **Earl Weaver,** Hall of Fame Manager, *FoxSports.com*, June 17th, 2014

"It just takes one little break here or there, and the momentum switches."

> — **Hunter Pence,** 4x All-Star and 2x World Series Champion, *MLB.com*, September 2nd, 2016

"I believe that momentum is a dangerous thing to rely on all the time, because it can change in a pitch or two."

> — **Aj Hinch,** World Series Championship Winning Manager, *Sportingnews.com*, October 18th, 2017

Key Principles

1. Remember: three-parts will and one-part skill.
2. Baseball games can be like a roller coaster: many highs, many lows... just hang on.
3. It's not how you start, but how you finish.

Riding the Waves

Picture this: A surfer sits out in the open ocean. The water is calm, and the surfer is in complete control. Atop his surfboard, the surfer can enjoy the tranquility of his surroundings. However, he has not come out to the open water for the tranquility. The surfer has ventured out in search of the big wave—the wave that will get his adrenaline pumping… the wave that will satisfy his craving for the thrill of competition… the wave that will push him towards his peak performance. He has come not for relaxation, but to embrace a challenge. The surfer sits patiently waiting for the biggest wave that may come his way. When the "big one" comes along, it will undoubtedly test his physical abilities, challenge his mental game, and for a moment leave the surfer wondering if he can withstand the momentum and pressure of the water. But if he does, and he stays on the board, and is able to ride the wave out, he will be ready for whatever comes up next.

Momentum shifts are unavoidable. It is just part of the rhythm. Just as waves in the ocean ebb and flow, the course of a game momentum constantly changes. This is a natural phenomenon, and the reason why we find baseball so entertaining. "Waves", momentum shifts, and adversity are a part of every game, and usually continually builds with each inning that passes by. It should be seen as a challenge, and as something to be embraced.

MLB pitcher Daniel Norris said, "I can't tell you how many times I've been sitting on my surfboard, waiting on a wave, and my mind just wanders to baseball. It's in the middle of the off-season and I'm out on the ocean, and I can't stop thinking about baseball." There are parallels between a surfer waiting for a big wave, and a baseball player competing in a game—consider this a type of "big wave". Just like the surfer, a ballplayer begins each game in control. They make the routine put outs in the field, and they make the pitches they are supposed to make to get each hitter out. But then—just like how a wave builds up behind a surfer in the open ocean—a change in momentum is bound to occur in a baseball game, and it usually can occur on just a single pitch. This is the natural evolution of every game. The wave is impossible to stop—and momentum is something that is out of your control. Although the momentum behind the "big wave" might be strong, it is your job as a player is to find a way to stay balanced on your board and ride it out.

A surfer may see a wave approaching far in the distance, just as a ballplayer might see a shift in momentum before it shows on the scoreboard. The "big wave" may show itself either as a letdown in one's own performance, i.e. booting a routine ground ball, walking the leadoff guy, striking out after a long at-bat; or as a boost in your opponent's game, i.e. they lead off an inning with back to back hits, their reliever gets out of a bases-loaded situation with a big strikeout, etc. Factors beyond the player's control, such as an umpire squeezing the strike zone, or the roar of the crowd, can also lead to a momentum swing. These situations are inevitable in each game. But given the player's level of awareness of the specific situation within each game, and his ability to sense the upcoming waves of momentum, he has the opportunity to mentally prepare himself to find a balance in his emotions, and to remain centered and calm. As Norris puts it, "Just the perspective of having to be calm and glide right into something as powerful as a wave and harness its power to catch it and ride it—it's so exhilarating, but mellow at the same time. It's this happy medium between being super intense, but completely relaxed." Just like the game of baseball!

Suppose the momentum shifts as your opponent hits a pitch right down the left field line, just out of the diving reach of the third basemen, in a crucial spot in the game. The only hope to get through the "wave" is to ride it out. The "wave" should not be viewed as a setback, or even an obstacle, but rather as an opportunity; an opportunity to test one's ability to remain focused, and in control of one's emotions. It is an opportunity to adapt and adjust one's game to what works best in changing situations.

But success can only be achieved if a player can proactively ride out the "wave" and stay above water. The goal is simply to stay afloat—nothing fancy, just keep grinding. Think about all the momentum shifts in Game 5 of the 2017 World Series between the Astros and Dodgers. The Astros went on to win 13 to 12 in 10 innings, in a game that featured 7 home runs, 4 lead changes, and 3 ties! In the game of baseball, momentum can shift on any single pitch, the question becomes: is the player able to stay balanced and centered, or has the building momentum and pressure of the "wave" thrown him off? If he stays balanced and centered, he is in a position to compete once the "wave", and momentum passes. However, if the player lets his emotions dictate his ability to adjust in the moment, he cannot stop thinking about a certain situation earlier in the game, or is flustered by the drastic turn of events, he will no longer be able keep his balance as momentum builds. He will continue to spiral out of control.

In the end, riding the "big wave" is the ultimate thrill. Just like a surfer, a ballplayer may struggle with the wave but stay on the board and ride it out. When a player stays calm under pressure, he can persevere no matter how big, or how many waves come his way. Once the player knows he can handle the waves and gets a feel for it, he can embrace even bigger waves, challenges, or situations he may encounter in pressure packed moments, late in games. Only through challenging oneself, and confronting increasingly bigger obstacles, can you improve.

Riding the Waves

WORKOUT

Hello–Goodbye Exercise

Pretend you are on the diamond. Each game and each inning will be an opportunity for you to embrace something (say hello), and an opportunity to let go of something (say goodbye). For example, say hello to nervousness of striking out and say goodbye to the fear of the result of your at-bat.

Now, as you imagine playing each inning, continue to fill in the blanks.

Inning 1 Hello: _nervousness_____ Goodbye: _fear of being judged_____

Inning 2 Hello:_____ Goodbye :_____

Inning 3 Hello:_____ Goodbye :_____

Inning 4 Hello:_____ Goodbye :_____

Inning 5 Hello:_____ Goodbye :_____

Inning 6 Hello:_____ Goodbye :_____

Inning 7 Hello:_____ Goodbye :_____

Inning 8 Hello:_____ Goodbye :_____

Inning 9 Hello:_____ Goodbye :_____

Extra Inning 10 Hello:_____ Goodbye :_____

Extra Inning 11 Hello:_____ Goodbye :_____

Extra Inning 12 Hello:_____ Goodbye :_____

Workout 27
Mental Point

Games are not the time to over analyze techniques or mechanics— it is the opportunity to simply play, by getting "outta your mind" and allowing the body to do what it has been trained to do.

Workout 27

Get Outta Your Mind:
It's the Only Way to Compete!

What the Pros Are Saying

"I try not to overthink … that's when I make the error and get myself in trouble. I try not to analyze things too much."

— **Nolan Arenado,** 4x Gold Glove and 3x Silver Slugger Award winner, *MLB.com,* April 26th, 2012

"When the game starts, you just have to use your athleticism and let the instincts take over."

— **Jimmy Rollins,** 4x Gold Glove winner and MVP, *NBCsports.com,* March 2nd, 2017

"There are going to be times when you're going to make mistakes. But you still have to be mentally able to focus… I feel like instincts get taken away from players now. We were taught to be our own coach at some points, and there are still times when you've got to understand that."

— **Josh Donaldson,** 3x All-Star and MVP, *Sportsnet.com,* October 14th, 2016

Key Principles
1. No one know you better than you; trust your instincts.
2. Overthinking leads to mistakes and miscues.
3. Listen carefully—your body knows what to do.

Get Outta Your Mind

We all have heard people say, "He's completely locked in, he's playing out of his mind!" Referring to someone who seems to make something happen every time he steps up to the plate. Have you ever performed "outta your mind" or felt completely locked in, pitching to perfection, going 4-for-4 at the plate, or making a few spectacular diving plays in the field? Maybe there is more to this "outta your mind" concept than meets the eye. Paradoxically, the idea is ultimately a metaphor for playing within yourself, where everything is effortless and smooth, where little thought occurs, and optimal performance just happens. In this workout, I will discuss how literally getting "outta your mind" is the best way to reach optimal personal peak performance on the diamond.

When athletes play "in their mind" they are not playing from instinct. They are over-thinking each situation; their thoughts are all over the place, and they over analyzing their mechanics. These thoughts interfere with their ability to perform. Further, their thoughts are in the past, on previous at-bats, or in the future—usually tied to expectations, outcome, and fears; everything they cannot control. Their thoughts are weighing them down much like an imaginary weight on their shoulders.

We all know what happens when this kind of mentality creeps in—the dreaded spiral in which a player loses control! Physically and mentally it looks like this: an initial loss of focus, fear about what might be or what is occurring, tensed arms, legs and shoulders, and an overwhelming feeling of anxiousness as the game speeds up. Then the poor play follows, usually an errant throw, or chasing a pitch in the dirt, or maybe a wild pitch. The only way to optimize performance is to play in the moment, and to respond to situations with calm awareness, as opposed to reacting out of fear and anxiety. I call this the "eye of the hurricane," calm on the inside, yet aware and active on the outside.

Veteran pitcher, Chad Bettis, said this about playing "outta his mind": "It is much more muted, almost to the extent where all you're listening to and all you're hearing is your heartbeat. All you're seeing and whatever you want to let in is happening." The key to staying in the moment is within all of us—the secret lies in our bodies. Our body is always in the present moment. When a baseball player becomes aware of his body, such as the rhythm when he swings, he simplifies things and enters a place of curiosity, simply noticing his present actions. This moves him away from distracting ego, fear, and anxiety-driven thoughts of over analyzing. In fact, all of the 'what-if,' 'shoulda,' or 'coulda' thoughts are no longer in the way, because the focus is on the pitch—observation rather than judgment. Essentially, by getting "outta your mind," you get "out of your way", and simply allow the techniques you have spent countless hours working on, either in the cage, on the field, or during throwing sessions, to just flow and perform effortlessly in the present.

So how can players shift their focus "outta their mind" (thoughts and judgments) and into their bodies (present moment)? It starts with a keen awareness; when you become aware of being submerged in over-thinking, fear, or that recognizable negative spiral, the idea is to simplify things, and shift attention to something in the present, and something you can control. For example, the athlete may focus on his breathing, or a place they feel calm and centered. 14- year veteran pitcher, Rich Hill, said, "It is all about staying in the moment, and executing when you're in that moment. That's all you can think about, and all you can control." This method of refocusing "outta your mind", and into your body, serves as a reconnection to the present—a place of calm and observation.

Game time is not the time to analyze technique or make adjustments that take the player out of their comfort zone—it is the opportunity to trust and execute. It is easy to let your mind get caught up in the results of your performance, get caught up in expectations, or think about a missed opportunity. Yet the aforementioned tools can help the player keep his attention "outta his mind", and in the present, able to respond to the moment and each pitch.

All athletes love those times when they feel immersed in the game, competing with great focus for sustained periods of time, and ultimately playing inside the zone. 2x All-Star and Silver Slugger Award winner, Shawn Green, in his book *The Way of Baseball*, talks about how he used the batting tee to focus on his breathing, get "outta his mind", and re-connect with his natural swing. Playing "outta your mind" slows the game down by taking the multiple thoughts that are racing through your head during each situation, and helps you focus what's necessary to perform at your best in that moment.

That Which Makes You Different Is What Makes You Special.

Get Outta Your Mind

WORKOUT

The Frog and the Centipede

*A frog was sitting on a patch of grass by his pond one sunny morning
when a large centipede passed by.
The frog watched this creature with fascination, then
said, "Excuse me, can I ask you a question?"
"Why, yes, of course," replied the centipede, pausing in his stride.
"I am amazed at the way you can proceed so harmoniously
with your one hundred legs," said the frog. "Can you explain
to me how you manage to keep them in order?"
The centipede reflected for a moment. "You know, I have never really
thought about it," he said. "Let me see if I can demonstrate it for you."
And he started to walk, thinking about which leg should follow another.
Immediately, he fell down and had great difficulty getting up again.
"You are dangerous!" he said to the frog angrily.
"Never again ask such questions!"*

After reading this poem, what does it make you aware of?

_____

_____

How does this relate to your game?

_____

_____

List three ways this insight will help your game:

1. _____

2. _____

3. _____

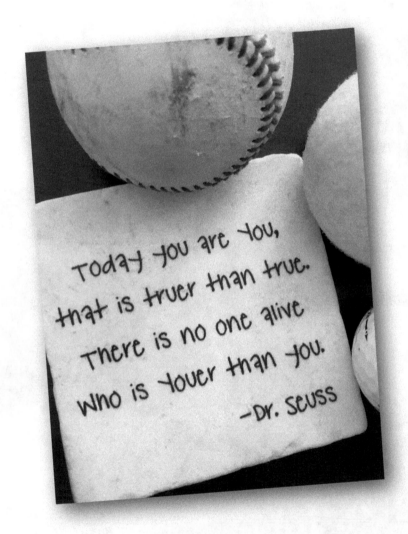

Today you are You,
that is truer than true.
There is no one alive
who is Youer than You.

—Dr. Seuss

Field of Dreams

Ramon and Santana observing Bobby.

Experimenting with grips.

Photo op at Pine Brook Baseball and Softball Academy.

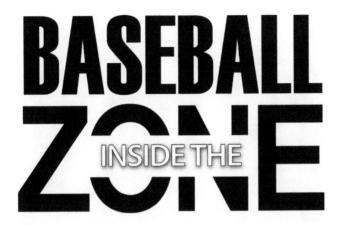

Section 4
POST-GAME WORKOUTS

Workout 28: Losing Stinks! *Dealing With a Tough Loss*..173

Workout 29: Mistakes, Setbacks and Failure: *Dealing With Disappointment*...................179

Workout 30: I'm Better! How Could I Lose! *7 Biggest Mistakes the Favorite Makes*...........185

Workout 31: Sweet Victory! *Seven Questions to Ask After a Win (or Loss)*.............................191

Workout 32: Flight, Fight, Freeze: *The Seven Biggest Fears That Paralyze Athletes*..............197

Workout 33: I Can't Believe I Choked! *Understanding Slumps, Blocks and the Yips*...........203

Post-Game Workouts

Don't Quit

When things go wrong, as they sometimes will,

When the road you're trudging seems all uphill,
When the funds are low and the debts are high,
And you want to smile, but you have to sigh,
When care is pressing you down a bit-
Rest if you must, but don't you quit.

Life is queer with its twists and turns,

As every one of us sometimes learns,
And many a fellow turns about
When he might have won had he stuck it out.
Don't give up though the pace seems slow -
You may succeed with another blow.

Often the goal is nearer than

It seems to a faint and faltering man;
Often the struggler has given up
When he might have captured the victor's cup;
And he learned too late when the night came down,
How close he was to the golden crown.

Success is failure turned inside out -

The silver tint in the clouds of doubt,
And you never can tell how close you are,
It might be near when it seems afar;
So stick to the fight when you're hardest hit -
It's when things seem worst that you must not quit.

- Author Unknown

Workout 28
Mental Point

How do you bounce back from a painful defeat? First off, let's acknowledge: It's not easy and it hurts!

Losing Stinks!
Five Steps to Dealing With a Tough Loss

What the Pros Are Saying

"You can say all the good things and motivate yourself, but at the end of the day, we're still human. It's still going to hurt."

— **Kelly Jansen,** 3x All-Star, *ESPN.com,* October 28th, 2018

"I don't like to ride the rollercoaster…If you respond to every bad game or tough game, you'll bounce around and ruin confidence in."

— **Aj Hinch,** World Series Winning Manager, *Yahoo Sports,* October 26th, 2017

"… There's been some sting to losing a couple of baseball games. There's been some difficult moments and there's also been a lot of opportunities to learn."

— **Gabe Kapler**, MLB Manager, *Yahoo Sports,* April 3rd, 2018

Key Principles
1. The only time you lose is when you don't learn.
2. Losing offers a fresh start.
3. Failure is feedback and part of the process.

Losing Stinks!

No one likes to lose in the regular season, and certainly no one likes to fail or lose in a post-season series. It's disappointing, frustrating, and sometimes feels like you let the opportunity of a lifetime slip right from between your fingers! Imagine being the 2011 Texas Rangers, who twice came within one strike of winning the World Series, giving up the lead in the 9th, 10th, and ultimately gave up a walk off homerun in the 11th inning of game 6. A baseball season is long, and there are going to be stretches throughout the season when the timing and rhythm as a player, and as a team, just doesn't seem to be clicking. The key is not allowing the losses or failures to dictate your emotions, and the process of the way you approach each game. Understand that each loss, mistake, setback, obstacle, and failure are inevitable. However, how teams and players adapt, adjust, and learn from these difficult experiences determines whether potential is fulfilled.

4x Gold Glove Award winner and MLB Manager, Mike Matheny, said, "For the last two weeks, we've been in a position to win almost every single game that we've been a part of here against some tough competition. And for some reason or another it's gotten away. Just one piece after another seems to be the key that particular night to not allow us from doing what we need to do." Every player and every team are disappointed by mistakes, setbacks, obstacles, and losing—in fact

they become even more frustrated when constantly replaying the games over in their head, trying to figure what went wrong. 2x All-Star, Carols Martinez, said, "It's frustrating, especially not to be able to put our finger on exactly what's going on." Losing is an inevitable part of their process, and you cannot allow disappointments to sidetrack you from striving towards the ultimate goal: continuous improvement and long-term success. Process the knowledge gained from each loss and shift the focus back to something that is in your control. Such as establishing how you can take the knowledge you've gained from each loss and incorporate it in your adjustments moving forward.

3x World Series Champion Manager, Bruce Bochy, said, "It was tough for everybody, trying to get on track. Losing wears on everybody. It's like any game or any tough streak, you've got to move on and focus forward." The key to moving forward after a tough loss, or a string of tough losses, is finding the excitement of the next opportunity. Each loss and setback represent the opportunity to grow and develop. Find the excitement in bringing the information you've gained from the loss, into the way you approach and make adjustments the next time you step in between the white lines.

The 2006 St. Louis Cardinals finished the regular season with an 83-78 record. They finished just a few games above .500 and managed to sneak into the postseason. This also included having the lowest win percentage of any team to make the playoffs that year, and despite losing 8 consecutive games twice throughout the season. Among those losing streaks Matheny said, "You can be frustrated all you want. But learning and talking it through about how we do it better is the challenge. Frustration is natural." It was clear that the Cardinals were able to learn from the loses and setbacks, and ultimately made them a more resilient and well- rounded team. They went on to capture a World Series Title, despite having the 3rd lowest win percentage in baseball history to make a postseason appearance!

Former MLB middle infielder, Zach Sorensen, said, "Often times when you talk about mental conditioning we talk about failure. It's such a big thing— failure in sports, failure in life— and how you respond to failure is a big deal. We often use the line that failure is only feedback. I even like to take it further than that and say failure is feedback and failure is also fuel to make you better."

You don't have to like losing, in fact you can even hate it more than you like to win! However, you must recognize it is inevitable, and necessary, for success. You deserve to be disappointed and even angry after a loss. However, this does not have to be a permanent state, and you do not have to waste your focus and energy pinpointing what went wrong. Rather, by utilizing a heightened awareness of what happened, you can begin to work through what knowledge you've gained form the loss, and how can you use that in the adjustments you make moving forward. You and your team may have played poorly today, or maybe you've played poorly for a few games in a row. However, one loss or a stretch of bad games does not define an entire season. Most teams and players panic and drastically alter their approach and routines when they experience a loss or a losing streak. It is important to understand that during this time your main opponent is yourself. Understand that you are a work in progress and not a fixed entity, this helps keep the door for improvement open!

The key point here is that winning is a process that is littered with setbacks, mistakes, obstacles, and failures. If processed correctly, an athlete will recognize these setbacks and losses as temporary. They can learn from them and ultimately move forward towards their goal. Don't be afraid to get back to the basics, or in other words— do the simple things better. The next time you lose, ask yourself: What can I learn from this? What can our team learn from this? How can I/we use this experience to make an adjustment in mechanics or approaches to reach the ultimate goal? Remember, behind every crisis lies a far more valuable opportunity.

Losing Stinks!

WORKOUT

"We made a bunch of mistakes tonight but I've also learned one other thing regarding baseball: 24 hours can make a huge difference. That's just one game. That's just one. We'll be back tomorrow… We'll be ready to play. We will not be affected mentally by tonight's game."

— **Joe Maddon**, World Series Winning Manager, *Baseballmentalgame.com.*

First off… let's acknowledge that it hurts to lose, especially when you have put yourself on the line and tried your best in that specific situation and time. Second, let's acknowledge that in baseball it's easy to fail, and hard to bounce back, but you can do it!

What was a time you or your team experienced a tough loss or a stretch of bad losses? Describe it:

_____

_____

_____

What are three things you and your team learned from those losses?

1. _____

2. _____

3. _____

How can you and your team use these lessons in future games?

_____

_____

_____

If you did, what would happen?

_____

_____

_____

 Workout 29
Mental Point

You don't have to like failure, in fact you can even hate it! However, you must recognize it is necessary for success. You deserve to be disappointed and even angry after a setback; however, this does not have to be a permanent state.

Mistakes, Setbacks and Failure:
Dealing With Disappointment

What the Pros Are Saying

"When I struggled, that was the first time I ever struggled, so I had to really figure out myself. It helped me understand what I need to do to continue my success and continue not to hit those low patches all the time. But when I do hit them, I know how to fix them."

— **Corey Seager,** Rookie of the Year Award Winner, 2x All-Star, *Dodgersnation.com*, October 10th, 2015

"The game is structured around you failing 7 out of 10 times. I understand that when it comes to baseball, you're going to fail. When it comes to life, you're going to fail. The key is you have to get back up and keep going. The more you can get back up and keep climbing that mountain, the better off you are in life, and in sports. You have to do it over and over and over again."

— **George Springer,** Silver Slugger Award Winner and World Series MVP, *MLB.com*, April 28th, 2014

Key Principles

1. Failure is feedback.
2. It's not how hard you can hit, but how hard you can get hit and bounce back.
3. It's not whether you make mistakes, but how you rebound.

Mistakes, Setbacks and Failure

Imagine this: You're playing in front of a sold-out crowd, grinding out a tough at-bat. You keep fouling off some tough pitches in on the hands. Then, you get frozen by a curveball, and get called out on strikes. Slowly you walk back to the dugout, frustrated that you weren't able finish off the at bat. Your mind begins to produce thousands of thoughts. What if I don't get another opportunity to contribute to help my team? What if I strikeout again in a similar situation? Your body becomes tense, and your focus is now stuck in a seesaw of thoughts that teeters between your last at-bat, and future situations in the game.

How can you get over this disappointment? Most often, we hear: just move on, focus on the next one. Don't you just hate those phrases? Still, that one at-bat seems to be eating away at you, and the only thing you can hear is the voice of doubt. As you walk back to the dugout, take off your helmet and batting gloves, pick up your hat and glove, you can feel the frustration building. In your mind, you are still replaying every pitch of the at-bat, as you carry the disappointment and frustration out into the field with you.

How do you cope with the disappointment? How do you bounce back from a defeat? First off, let's acknowledge: It's not easy and it hurts! However, we must learn to let the pain go as quickly as possible, because it becomes imperative to reset your focus on to the next pitch. Imagine how hard it

is to be successful on the next pitch if you are carrying the burden of the defeat from the previous pitch! Each player must learn to take the information gained from being unsuccessful and apply it towards making adjustments. What must you do next time to get better? How will you take advantage of certain situations, and continually put yourself in a better position? Let your failures be the groundwork for your adjustments!

The following are five steps to help you process your failure as a way of benefiting your performance on the next pitch. Equally so, this list is great for parents, coaches, and friends as they try to support the player during the process of disappointment, release, and re-adjustment.

1. A right to be disappointed: You've earned the right to be disappointed. Let's face it: after putting in all the work in the cages and in practice fine tuning your craft, and competing with all your heart, it seems practically impossible to simply just let it go. It's okay to be disappointed. In fact, it's even expected. Why wouldn't you be? Disappointment is a natural emotion—it even hurts, and that's okay too, as long as you learn from it. Failure is something that is out of your control. In fact, it is inevitable. Give yourself a second to decompress and feel your feelings. Then, begin to channel the energy into information that will help put you in a better position to be successful on the next pitch.

2. One step closer: Believe it or not, you are actually one step closer to your goals! Hall of Fame pitcher, John Smoltz, said, "I think it's pretty clear that my career wasn't all about talent. I wasn't' sprinkled with any magic dust. I wasn't the fastest or the strongest, or even the smartest…. A lot of my success was achieved by constantly learning, adapting, and overcoming obstacles." Smoltz talked about learning from the hitter's last swing and making adjustments to increase his chance of success when he stepped back on the rubber. You can do the same. He said, "The greater I fail, the more I learned. I reinvented myself. Making adjustments gave me one more opportunity to win." Don't accept failure, learn from it!

3. Failure provides feedback: If you listen, you become aware. Failures, setbacks, and obstacles always seem to derail us from the way we approach the game, but it is your job as a player to readjust and embrace feedback. Feedback should be viewed without judgment, and as a learning opportunity in which you can make changes and adapt—to adjust to the next situation or the next pitch. Think about it: Was there ever a perennial all-star, or championship caliber team that didn't learn from failures, setbacks, and obstacles? Know why you are competing, and use your big "Big Why", from Workout #3, to get yourself back on track. Knowing why you

play is like constantly adding fuel to the fire inside of you to compete and succeed. Use failure as feedback, and your "Big Why," to constantly keep the fire blazing!

4. Reframe it! Simply stated, as you step out of the box or off the mound, and as you process the last pitch, ask yourself the basic questions. Even though I may have missed the last pitch, what did I learn? What adjustments can I make? And don't forget: Give yourself some credit for showing up and putting yourself on the line. How many others are competing with such a heart as yours?

5. Focus on the process, not the outcome. This is probably the most important point, and the one that all other points can probably be folded into. Legendary Texas Longhorns coach Auggie Garrido said, "It's about the process. You have to stay within the framework of the process to be consistent. Be connected to the process and be connected to being a ballplayer… Players should focus on the process because the process is something they can control, rather than the outcome, which they never had control over." The confidence Garrdio refers to is built through the process of failure. Consistent confidence in baseball is built through processing the information you gained from failure and channeling it into how you adjust and adapt to the next pitch.

Mistakes, Setbacks and Failure

WORKOUT

"The truth is, one of the keys to my success has been how well I've handled failure."

— **John Smoltz**, Hall of Fame Pitcher, <u>Starting and Closing: Perseverance, Faith, and One More Year</u>, By: John Smoltz and Don Yaeger

A mistake, setback, or failures are never the problem. The problem lies when we do not learn and adjust from our Mistakes. Mistakes provide feedback.

Next time you make a mistake in between the white lines, try not to judge it or yourself. Be aware of what happened and let it go. Trust yourself to make an adjustment the next time you're in the same situation.

List three mistakes you made in the last game you played:

1. _____

2. _____

3. _____

Choose one, and describe how you judged yourself at the time.

_____

_____

_____

_____

What do you notice when you talk to yourself this way?

_____

_____

_____

_____

What could you say to yourself after a mistake that would be helpful?

_____

_____

_____

_____

_____

_____

_____

_____

Create a Mistake Ritual. What short routine could you do to help yourself let go of mistakes? Describe it.

_____

_____

_____

_____

_____

_____

_____

_____

_____

_____

Workout 30
Mental Point

It's important to remember that you must focus on the present, compete, and let go of uncontrollable expectations. Keep the game simple!

I'm Better—How Could I Lose!
7 Biggest Mistakes the Favorite Makes

What the Pros Are Saying

"I want us to be uncomfortable. The moment you get into your comfort zone after having such a significant moment in your life like that [winning the World Series], the threat is that you're going to stop growing."

> — **Joe Maddon,** *Chicago Tribune*, February 12th, 2017

"If you buy into the hype, if you buy into the nonsense of it, that's when you set yourself up for failure. Just try to play good baseball. Just worry (focus) about making a pitch or having a good at-bat or fielding a ball or catching a fly ball."

> — **John Lester,** 3x World Series Champion and NLCS MVP, *The Mercury News*, August 21st, 2014

"Don't read any articles. Don't listen to any TV shows. Just focus on the 25 men in that clubhouse. You're just playing to win, and you're playing as a team."

> — **Kevin Millar,** World Series Champion, *Boston.com*, October 8th, 2017

Key Principles

1. Winning isn't just about technique, it's about how you compete.
2. Perfection is rarely required to win.
3. Let go of expectations: they can't be controlled.

I'm Better—How Could I Lose!

Imagine this: It's the championship game of a Memorial Day tournament. This is a well-known tournament with teams coming from all over the country to compete. Your lineup is stacked, and all your pitchers have great stuff. Your team is respected. You beat your opponent in the first game, now they look sluggish. As you and your teammates watch your opponent warm up and get lose, you start to think, "This is going to be an easy win."

The game does not go as expected. Your team brought a sense of over confidence into the game, and as a result, you are not as mentally sharp. Your approach at the plate is different than the approach that got you there in the first place. Your hitters are overaggressive, and everyone is over swinging, trying to hit a home run on every pitch, which results in many routine fly balls and weak groundballs. As you enter the 7th inning of the game, you look up at the scoreboard, and realize that your team is down 2-0. Costly errors in the field, and unfocused approaches at the plate have cost your team. The other team is battling and executing, and you are now in a dogfight. Your team is being outplayed in all areas of the game, including the mental side of it!

All players and teams have probably experienced this situation at least once in their baseball career. Yet how many of these players really seek to understand what happened, and try to put a plan together so

that history doesn't repeat itself in another game down the road?

This workout will highlight some of the biggest *mistakes* a favorite can make against a supposed underdog.

1. Overconfidence: How many players have you seen start a game feeling like they are entitled to win based on where they stand in the standings? The downfall with such a mindset is that focusing on off the field factors will take a player out of the present moment, and distract them from executing pitch to pitch adjustments.

2. Focus on winning: We all want to win! However, it's important to remember that winning is not 100% in our control. Whenever a player or team begins to think ahead to the result or the outcome, attention is taken away from the pitch that is about to be delivered, and is focused on something that is out of their control. Players must recognize when this happens and bring their attention back to the process of the present moment—on something they can control. It might start with focusing on their breath and getting themselves in a centered and relaxed place (See Workout 11, "How to Play in the Moment: It's as Easy as Breathing").

3. Listen to the hype: Your friends, teammates, coaches, scouts, and maybe even the media are going to praise you. While these accolades are nice to hear, they will not help you execute on the next pitch. All your effort should be on what you can do to prepare for each game. This mindset isn't glamorous, but if you listen to some of the game's greats, this is how they approach each game. They focus only on what they can control, such as their routines, and the process of establishing a clear mind to be ready to make proper in-game adjustments.

4. Rely on talent alone: Talent is great—it makes the sport easier to learn for some than for others, and it helps players get away with some flaws in their game. However, everyone will eventually face a pitcher, batter, or team in which talent alone isn't enough to earn the win. In fact, hype often is direct result of talent. When a player "buys into the hype," he starts to believe that his talent alone is enough to be successful on the diamond. Talent, work ethic, on-field intelligence, and the will to *compete* are all crucial factors in developing as a player.

5. Lack competitive intensity: What percentage of the game is about competing, and what percentage is about playing your best? It's at least 50/50, no? On a day to day basis competing is more important than playing your best. It's extremely rare that someone is able to play his best all the time. However, a player can always control how he competes. This is where the focus needs to be.

6. Lose composure: Sure, if you're the favorite, everybody is expecting you to win. Therefore, when things get close, the underdog is inspired and momentum seems to be swung in their favor. For you, the frustration kicks in. Before you know it, the negative self-talk starts, and suddenly frustration gets carried out to the field, which usually is followed up by an error on a routine play. The favorite always has to be prepared to give their best effort, remain focused, and battle to execute on every pitch, no matter the quality of the team they are competing against.

7. No awareness: Oftentimes, the favorite is not even aware of what's happening on the field regarding their approach and adjustments. This is particularly the case because they have a preconceived notion of how each at-bat, and the game, is going to play out. Once again, their focus is on the past or future, and they are essentially playing to the level of their competition. It's important to enter each game without expectations, except that you will compete fully and trust the process of your in-game approach.

As a favorite, it's important to remember that you must focus on the present, compete, and let go of uncontrollable expectations.

I'm Better—How Could I Lose!

WORKOUT

When an athlete focuses on what he cannot control, stress goes up, breathing increases, muscles tighten, confidence falls, performance lowers, and slumps continue to build... this is because you have no direct control over these things. They change from pitch to pitch.

When a ballplayer focuses on what they can control, they will be more positive, relaxed, and open to making proper adjustments. This is because the process is within their control.

Peak performance demands that an athlete focus on what they can control.

<u>List controllables and uncontrollables for your next game.</u>

CONTROLLABLES	UNCONTROLLABLES
preparation	*weather (sun/wind/rain)*

What does completing the above table make you aware of?

_____

_____

_____

How can you use it to help you?

_____

_____

What are the main three uncontrollables that that you lose your focus on?

1. _____

2. _____

3. _____

What happens when you lose your focus?

_____

_____

When you lose your concentration, what controllables could you re-focus on?

_____

_____

Imagine changing your focus to something on your list that you can control. How do you think that could help?

_____

_____

What would if take to make that concentration change?

_____

_____

Is it worth doing? _____

Workout 31
Mental Point

Whether a player wins or loses, fails or succeeds, he should always ask himself some key questions about his performance. The goal of asking questions is to raise awareness of what happened, so you can analyze your performance and that of your opponent.

Sweet Victory!
Seven Questions to Ask After a Win (or Loss)

What the Pros Are Saying

"Competing at the highest level is not about winning. It's about preparation, courage, understanding, and nurturing your people and heart. Winning is the result."
— **Joe Torre,** 4x World Series Winning Manager and Hall of Famer, *USAtoday.com*, February 9th, 2016

"If you're not willing to learn, then I firmly believe you're not going forward."
— **Dallas Keuchel,** Cy Young Award Winner, World Series Champion, *Foxsports.com*, February 26th, 2018

"When you put everything, every ounce of your being into something and you come up short, it hurts, and it's supposed to hurt... You can't look back. We don't talk about last year, we don't talk about next week. We talk about today and we talk about the next game. That's all we can really control."
— **Dave Roberts,** Manager of the Year Award Winner, *CNBC.com*, November 2nd, 2017

Key Principles
1. Little successes add up to big wins.
2. Win or lose, you can always learn from your performance.
3. The only loss is when you don't learn.

Sweet Victory!

Sometimes after winning a game, especially a close game, players get satisfied with the win, and simply move on to the next game without evaluating their performance. This is not the time to take your foot off the gas, but to stay grounded, humble, and continue to improve and build on what adjustments are working, and analyze what's not working.

Many coaches like to say that you learn more from your losses than from your wins. Certainly, this can be true. Oftentimes, losses do stand out more, and we tend to focus more intently on the things that we did wrong, which in turn forces you to understand how things did not go according to plan. However, don't be fooled: as much information that we typically walk away with after a loss can be taken from a win as well. Remember that winning or losing is out of your control. Because of this, the smart player goes beyond the box score, and looks to continue to build upon the process of his development despite the outcome of the game.

By analyzing your performance and that of your opponent, players will begin to better understand what routines, approaches, and adjustments need to stay the same, and what needs to change in their game.

The remainder of this workout will highlight seven key questions that players should ask themselves after a hard-fought win, or a tough loss.

1. Briefly describe the score and the overall feel of the game: This is simply a question for the player to log the score and write down their overall impressions of the game. It might be as simple as, "I went 2-3 at the plate, with a strikeout, a walk, and an RBI. I did a good job of being on time for the fastball, but I was out in front on off-speed pitches." This question is not to be judgmental, but simply to note the objective facts about different situations throughout the game.

2. How did I feel mentally and physically coming into the game? It's important to understand how you felt in order to assess where you need to go. Mental and physical fatigue are factors that often influence a player's routines and how he prepares, so they should be noted. Understanding these issues will help a player be aware of the situation and make the proper adjustments if necessary.

3. What are three things I did well? Hall of Fame Outfielder, Tony Gwynn, said, "Knowing the strike zone is very important, but I think the first thing is knowing yourself, knowing the things you do well." It's important to identify our strengths and understand what our focal points are, mechanically, so that we can replicate them at the plate or on the mound. This awareness will provide feedback to continue building on strengths. In the 140-year history of Major League Baseball, there have only been 23 perfect games pitched, and only 18 players have hit 4 homeruns in a game. Typically, there is no such thing as a perfect performance. However, there is also no such thing as a completely flawed performance. It is always somewhere in between. Our job in competition is to create a situation where we put ourselves in a position to do our best and compete.

4. What are three things which I can improve on? There are always different areas of your game that you can further develop and improve. You just have to refocus and not get complacent. Success does not just happen! It comes from preparation, acknowledgement, awareness, and a commitment to improve.

5. If I played this opponent again, what would I do the same, and what would I do differently? This question will help you adjust, and adopt a game plan, to keep you ahead of your opponent. All-Star pitcher Yovani Gallardo, said, "Obviously that third time (facing a lineup) is a bit different because they've seen a lot more pitches. They make adjustments. Any time you see a hitter making an adjustment, you have to make an adjustment as well and try to interrupt that timing that he has. They've seen a lot of pitches throughout the game, so you want to mix certain things up." Success Is not achieved through a cookie-cutter approach. Something that worked once, may not work again. Players must be willing to adopt and adjust their game to each pitch, count, and situation in a game.

6. What are my next steps? Who can help me? This is an important question as it makes the player think about what he needs to do next, and subsequently who could help him get to the next step. It might be a short-term answer to help him prepare for the next competition, or a long-term one to help him prepare for the next level in his development.

7. How do I feel about my effort and play regarding the game? Again, this is a self-reflection question. It's an opportunity for the player to simply identify where he is at mentally and physically. An answer might be, "I'm mentally and physically exhausted, but feel good about my effort and the adjustments I made. I feel confident that my mechanics and my technique in the field are where I want, and need, them to be heading into the next game."

In summary, by documenting your games and progress, the information will serve as a reference point towards your ongoing development, and will allow players see tendencies and patterns in which they can make necessary adjustments. Remember, if the result is a sweet victory... congratulations! If it's a tough loss... tomorrow is another opportunity!

Sweet Victory!

WORKOUT

Seven Questions to Ask After a Win (or Loss)

Date:_____

Single game ☐	Tournament ☐	Turf field ☐	Day game ☐
Double header ☐	League game ☐	Grass field ☐	Night game ☐

Game location / weather:

_____

Opponent's team name:

_____

Won ☐   Lost ☐

Score:_____

Overall record vs. opponent:_____

1. Describe the game:

_____

_____

_____

_____

2. How did I feel mentally and physically coming into the game?

_____

_____

_____

3. What are three things I did well?

- _____
- _____
- _____

4. What are three things I didn't do well which I can improve on?

- _____
- _____
- _____

5. If I played this opponent again, what would I do the same? What would I do differently?

_____

_____

_____

_____

6. What are my next steps to making these adjustments? Who can help me?

_____

_____

_____

_____

7. How did I feel about my effort and play regarding the game?

_____

_____

_____

_____

Workout 32
Mental Point

Anyone who has experienced an injury understands that the mental scars don't just disappear when the doctor says that you're cleared to play.

Flight, Fight, Freeze:
The Seven Biggest Fears That Paralyze Athletes

What the Pros Are Saying

"You cannot allow baseball to become your entire life, your complete identity. As wonderful as the game is, and as much as you love this sport, you also need to work on developing yourself as a person."

> — **Rick Ankiel,** Rookie of the Year Award finalist, *The Players Tribune*, September 28th, 2017

"Athletes are used to seeing themselves as warriors able to withstand multiple physical challenges, and have battled to get to the next level because of their mental and physical toughness…Now they may be sidelined by an enemy they can't even see: their mind."

> — **Dr. Janet Taylor,** *With No One Looking, a Hurt Stays Hidden, NY Times*, October 29th, 2012

Key Principles
1. The athlete is a person first and a performer second.
2. Choking happens! What's important is your response
3. Our biggest fears come out when we feel most vulnerable.

Flight, Fight, Freeze

How many times have you heard the following from a coach, parent, or teammate: "If only he played to his potential..." "If only he could play like he practices"... "He hits well in batting practice, but it doesn't translate to the game"... "If only he wouldn't get so anxious in late game situations"..."If only he would stop thinking so much, and just let his instincts take over".... "He is so much better than this, but..." and so on and so forth? We all know the mental side of baseball is huge. Noted sports psychologist, Riley Nickols, said, "A baseball player's mental game can be his biggest asset or biggest hindrance to cultivating robust self-confidence and achieving consistent performance. In baseball, there is a significant amount of time between pitches, innings, and games where players have an opportunity to think and reflect on past or future performance. The ability to remain present and engaged in the current moment will best allow an athlete to notice and respond more effectively to both internal and external cues."

The game is made up of four parts: technical, strategic, physical, and mental. One of these parts without the others makes it impossible to reach full potential. You can think of it like a car. The technical part is the body—a stable foundation, streamlined to make the car travel smoothly. The strategic part is the steering wheel—able to travel in the desired direction or change course whenever necessary. The physical part is the gas—physical preparation and stamina, the component ensuring that the car has the juice to complete the journey. The mental part is the engine—the most essential component, the force that starts the car and makes it run. When all of the above are working smoothly together, the player's game on the field runs smooth. Yet, when one of the components goes wrong, the car breaks down and the player's game does not run as smoothly.

Knowing all of this, the key question becomes: What gets in the way of a player performing well in pressure filled situations? More often than not, it is a result of different fears that blocks the path of success. Oftentimes, the player is aware of these fears but does not accept them, creating an internal struggle. It is during these times that we see pitchers struggling to find their command, and hitters over anxiously swinging at pitches out of the strike zone. Other times, the fears may be just below their conscious thought patterns, and in this case, it becomes necessary to delve a bit deeper into what is actually behind the fears. The following are seven of the biggest fears that can hold a player back from achieving his best.

1. Fear of Not Being Good Enough: This fear rears its head all the time, both on and off the field; in fact, just thinking about it may trigger an "ah-ha" moment. We all want to believe in ourselves and our abilities to perform at a high level, and anything short of that can be disheartening. In games, players sometimes second guess themselves, and begin to fear that they are not good enough to put together a good at-bat; they then lose their will and compete less than 100%. Sometimes in life, and baseball, setbacks may seem like a validation of not being good enough—that we lack what it takes to make it to the next level. However, while we may have setbacks, what really determines who we are as a person, and player, is how we respond to them.

2. Fear of Failure: 5x World Series champion and World Series MVP, Derek Jeter, said, "I was not afraid to fail. I failed in spring training, in the regular season, in the postseason, and in the World Series, but you have to have the ability to separate one day from the next." The fear of failure usually comes to the forefront of most player's thoughts during pressure situations. Usually the player feels an overwhelming expectation to succeed in the moment. The player is afraid to fail because he directly associates who he is as a player, and person, based off how he performs on the field. Additionally, he may be afraid of what others think if he does not play to his potential. Often times a player is afraid to experiment, afraid to try make mechanical adjustments, or afraid to take a risk; his fear of failure is the cause.

3. Fear of the Unknown: This fear comes about in preparation for a big game. The player can't possibly know for sure whether he will win or lose. This fear of the unknown creates a high-level of anxiety about what's going to happen. Essentially, players are creating hypothetical situations in their head that they feel may play out throughout the course of the game. Just like the outcome, these hypotheticals are something that the player cannot control. When a hitter fears the unknown, he walks to the plate without an approach, simply swinging without any regard for a plan, because he is uncomfortable standing in the box. Being aware that he is uncomfortable in the situation, and accepting the moment, will allow him to make adjustments that put him in a better position to be successful, rather than giving into the emotions of the fear of the unknown. For example, the hitter may adopt a two-strike approach at the beginning of the at-bat, taking the attention away from the fear of the unknown, and focusing on something simple, like not trying to do too much, and just getting the barrel to the ball to make hard contact.

4. Fear of Being Judged: This often comes up when a player is thinking about what parents, coaches, teammates, or even scouts are thinking as he is playing. The player feels every little aspect of the game is being viewed under a microscope, starting from how he warms up, to how he performs in all areas of the game on the field. This simple loss of concentration takes the player away from staying focused in the moment of each pitch, and towards something they can't control—like the opinions of all individuals outside the white lines. It is here that unconditional acceptance from the support team is so important. When such support is provided, the player can feel calm, relaxed, and focused in the moment.

5. Fear of Not Meeting Expectations: This is similar to the fear of being judged, in that, the player cannot control what someone else expects. Professional baseball players often feel the burden to play to the back of their baseball card. There can be an assumed expectation that players must be able to either consistently duplicate the stats they have put up in the past or exceed them. This expectation only leaves the players feeling that there are two types of results: failure or success. The process (journey) is ignored. For a player to play his best, he must be in the present and focus on the experience. Focusing on expectations of success, or failure, creates a mental distraction and hinders a player's ability to process information on each pitch.

6. Fear of Success: This fear manifests itself when a player, for example, has gone 2 for 2 at the plate and then begins to think, "I shouldn't be getting a hit off this pitcher – he's throwing way too hard" Or the pitcher may buy into the "hype" that surrounds the hitter he is facing, and therefore feel undeserving of striking out the "homerun king." Other times, the uncertainty and subsequent anxiety of putting themselves on the line for possible success is too much to handle. The certainty of losing, while disappointing, is well-known, and a familiar road already traveled. Players often think that with a certain game's success, that they must "live up" to that performance each time they step onto the diamond. The pressure to perform increases. They start to overthink about living up to those expectations and the stress it entails, and as a result, they ultimately fear becoming successful.

7. Fear of Injury or Re-Injury: This fear is driven by our macho sports culture's stigma, and unwillingness to deal with the emotional stress and traumatic experiences that may result from injuries. Specifically neglected is the athlete's uncertainty about recovery, alienation from the team, fear of not being able to return at full strength, and even anxiety about what might happen should the situation recur. For example, pitcher Tyler Chatwood said this in his first game back from Tommy John surgery, "I got nervous before every game, but this was different… Am I really ready for this?" It's important to note that while doctors may clear a baseball player physically, the player still may not have processed through the fear emotionally. Anyone who has experienced an injury understands how the mental scars don't just disappear when the doctor says you're cleared to play.

In today's sporting society, exhibiting any sign of weakness or fear is difficult for a player. Society views vulnerability as weakness, whereas in reality, awareness of vulnerability equates to true strength. Fears like the seven mentioned above appear all the time, especially in pressure packed situations. They are all a type of defense mechanism used to prevent players from feeling comfortable on the mound, at the plate, or in the field. Yet, recognizing such fears and having the courage to work through them is what truly enables players to grow, and reach their individual potential.

Flight, Fight, Freeze

WORKOUT

The Seven Biggest Fears That Paralyze Athletes

Rate these fears in order of how they affect you:

_____ Fear of not being good enough   _____ Fear of not meeting expectations

_____ Fear of failure   _____ Fear of success

_____ Fear of the unknown   _____ Fear of injury/re-injury

_____ Fear of being judged   _____ other (did I miss one?)

Choose the top fear and write it down.

_____

When you think of this fear, what do you experience?

_____

_____

What is the scariest aspect about that fear?

_____

On a scale of 1 to 10 (10 being the most), how strong is the fear?_____

How do you experience the fear on the diamond (i.e. tense/over anxious)?

_____

Where do you feel the fear in your body?

_____

Now, bring your attention to a time on the field when you felt calm. How did you experience it?

_____

Where do you feel the calm in your body?

_____

Now, take a minute to notice the calm.

Go back to noticing the fear... how do you experience it now?

_____

_____

Usually the fear will subside.

Workout 33
Mental Point

We often forget that behind the all-star's exterior, the athlete is a person first and a baseball player second.

I Can't Believe I Choked!
Understanding Slumps, Blocks and the Yips

What the Pros Are Saying

"There are things in your personal life that have an impact, and even though you may not want them to, they can affect your game."

— **Nelson Cruz,** *USA Today*, July 5th, 2017

"I've been struggling so much with my private life…going out on the field? I couldn't do it anymore because I was so overwhelmed. The stuff I was dealing with finally seeped its way onto the game."

— **Joey Votto,** *Bleacherreport.com*. June 24th, 2009

Key Principles

1. When athletes walk between the white lines, their experiences, fears, and traumas follow them.
2. Trust yourself, trust your game, trust your process
3. Everyone chokes. It's what you do next.

I Can't Believe I Choked!

How many times have you seen ballplayers tense up, get over anxious, and underperform, or choke in a big spot, on a big stage? In practice, they play great—not a care in the world, and complete confidence in their abilities. Yet once the game starts, begin to look mechanical like a robot. Perhaps a pitcher can't find the zone at all, as his pitches keep getting by the catcher and hitting the back stop. Or maybe a routine throw in the field becomes unmanageable. Fans become dumbfounded, and cannot believe that an elite athlete seems human, and that they can succumb to this type of pressure. "How can this happen? What's the cause of this?"

In looking for the solution, many coaches, fans, players, media, and even performance experts start by critiquing what they can see (i.e. wild pitches, unable to make routine throws, or even spiked balls in the dirt on a pickoff throw). Their initial intent is to look above the surface to find what's broken in hopes of a mechanical "quick fix." Certainly, this may be the place to look if the situation occurs once or twice. However, if the choke, slump, or yip continues repeatedly under pressure, it falls in the category of a repetitive sports performance block.

A repetitive sports performance block (i.e. choke, slump, yips) is actually the _symptom_ of an underlying issue. The _cause_ is an accumulation of negative experiences (traumas) from which the athlete has not been able to move on. In actuality, this block has little to do with the last time the player "choked." Rather, something about that pressure situation was the trigger that brought the unprocessed issue to the surface, where it distracted the athlete's performance. Players often experience underlying nervousness and anxiety and try to hide or resist it.

Oftentimes, the athlete doesn't want to address his anxiety for fear of being judged by teammates or fans. Former MLB pitcher and outfielder, Rick Ankiel, said, "… Millions of people just saw me throw a wild pitch. Then you'll think about your family watching the game, and your friends… and your teammates, and your manager… you'll think of the people you're letting down." Other times, the athlete may be completely unaware of the root cause of his anxiety, since it has been disassociated from his consciousness in an effort to protect his personal psyche. He typically will spend countless hours attempting every drill he can imagine, and any outlet he can think out to fix his issues.

Much like "heavy baggage" we hold onto on a daily basis, these negative experiences can grip a person, and accumulate during a person's life from both on- and off-field incidents. Emotional trauma can come from situations such as embarrassment; from dropping a routine fly ball, or repeatedly missing the strike-zone and walking hitters.

Physical trauma can derive from getting hit by a pitch, Tommy John surgery, maybe even a knee injury after hitting the base the wrong way. Additionally, off-field trauma can occur and accumulate stemming from issues such as divorce, death, car accidents, or other circumstances. Similarly, excessive judgment, and expectations, from parents, coaches, media, scouts, or yourself can also unknowingly add weight to the burden of pressure.

Throughout our lives, we encounter physical and emotional trauma. Depending upon the severity of these instances and our preparedness to meet them at the time, we sometimes absorb and process through these encounters, and other times we do not. When we are unable to process these experiences, the stress does not just disappear over time. Unlike physically recovering from Tommy John surgery, there is no set timetable in which a player can return to performing on the field. Rather, we store the unprocessed memory in the brain/body, where it may show itself at unexpected times.

These unprocessed negative experiences can accumulate, just like refilling the bucket after a round of batting practice. Emotional/physical trauma-like experiences get held in the body's central nervous system. They directly interfere with the athlete's ability to access and adapt to situations and perform movements that were once so easy and instinctual. Finally, when a ball tumbles out of the bucket, the player's repetitive sports performance block is now on public display for all to see, judge, and evaluate. Worst of all, it creates an overwhelming sense of self-doubt. Outfielder, Khris Davis, said, "The creature is what I call doubts inside yourself that bubble up, right to the surface of your consciousness, when you're performing a certain action. It's that tiny voice inside you that somehow takes over at times whether you like it or not. It's a million negative thoughts—not even necessarily fully formed, but just present—they appear at the worst possible moment. It saps all of your confidence when you're about to do something that you know you're fully capable of doing well."

In summary, it's clear that we hold emotional (fears) and physical (injuries) trauma-like experiences in our bodies. As a person, this "baggage" can consciously or unconsciously affect how we react, adapt, and adjust to everyday situations. As a player, it can also carry onto the diamond, and affect the athlete's ability to perform. In light of this, it makes sense to look beyond the surface of the slump, choke, or yips, to find the cause of it at its root. The athlete is not broken, or a "head case," as some might suggest. The block is part of the process, and actually can be a valuable clue to turning the situation around. Ultimately, the athlete will emerge mentally stronger, move without hesitation, and compete with increased confidence in himself as a person, and as a player.

I Can't Believe I Choked!

WORKOUT

Think of a time you choked or got really uptight... when was it? Where was it? Who were you playing?

_____

_____

_____

_____

What did you try to do at the time to try and manage the situation?

_____

_____

_____

_____

Describe in detail what happened, and what you experienced...

Before:_____

_____

_____

During:_____

_____

_____

After:_____

_____

_____

Baseball Inside the Zone™

Has it happened in another area of your life, on or off the field? Describe it.

_____

_____

_____

_____

_____

_____

Recognizing the above, what does this make you aware of?

_____

_____

_____

_____

_____

_____

What are three things you could try next time as you feel yourself starting to get tense?

1. _____

2. _____

3. _____

Conclusion

What's Next?

Baseball Inside the Zone is intended to stimulate ideas, thoughts, and questions. Ultimately the workbook is intended to provide a foundation to help you become more self-aware, present minded, and to embrace the mental edge over the course of your baseball journey. Like any journey, different events, experience, and situations throughout each game will bring different insights—be aware of these insights and continually build on them.

Baseball Inside the Zone is meant to continually evolve, bring you back to a centered place, and slow the game down, no matter where you are in your baseball career. Because of this, I encourage you to revisit and reassess the workouts throughout your journey. Joe Maddon preaches that the "process is fearless", let go of the outcome, and focus on the things you can control that aid your development as a player. The process must be encountered with patience, purpose, and perseverance. Remember, the process is a journey, and it takes one step at a time without being afraid to fail.

Now that you have read and experienced *Baseball Inside the Zone*, I thank you for your time and hope you have found it both rewarding and thought-provoking. Please share with me your insights, experiences, successes, failures, obstacles, and set-backs. I genuinely look forward to reconnecting in my future books, workshops, or consultations.

My Next Step...

As I mentioned, like your personal journey, mine is also evolving. In the Introduction I mentioned how this book started with my clients asking me questions related to mental training. Little did I know at the time that it would eventually lead to me publishing my second book!

But as we know, no journey is complete without the next step... My next step is to choose certain key chapters and expand on them in another book. With this in mind, I have already begun writing a book called Winning from the Inside Out: More than an athlete person first. Every time. Additionally, I am looking to increase my social media presence and create a 'More Than an Athlete' podcast and blog. Stay tuned.

The reward is in the process.

B'simcha (with happiness)

Rob

Rob

P.S. If you want to chat more, share an idea, experience, or thought, agree or disagree with something I said, please contact me at:

- rob@insidethezone.com
- www.insidethezone.com
- 973-723-0314

I'll look forward to hearing from you!

"If you are an athlete wanting to take your game to the next level on and off the field or as I like to say getting an edge however you can. Baseball Inside the Zone is the book to get. I believe baseball is one of the most mentally tough games to play. So that being said I have also played at the highest level and I know what it takes. Talent can only take someone so far. You have to have the work ethic and most importantly the mental toughness/mental skills to make it to the big leagues and be successful at that level. I have personally worked with Rob for a number of years and I have done many of these exercises myself. Rob has helped me tremendously, and I am forever grateful for the time he has spent with me and our friendship we have. The way he breaks each chapter down is so important and will really help athletes of all ages understand the concepts."

- Steve Lombardozzi, MLB Player

"Baseball Inside the Zone will help players of all ages stay focused and concentrate on what's important. The 33 individual workouts are a great way for players, coaches, and teams to practice their mental game. I have known Rob for 10 years and have seen his personal commitment to athletes of all levels and sports. Speaking as a Major League Baseball player and now coach, I highly recommend Baseball Inside the Zone if your looking to gain the mental edge."

- Mackey Sasser, former MLB Player

"Rob's book "Baseball Inside the Zone" reminds us that mire individuals must deal with success and failure knowing that such a fine line exists between the two. The more you understand what you can control, the closer to that successful fine line! "Baseball Inside the Zone" is a must read for any player at all levels. As a former MLB"er and now coach, I use Rob's workouts all the time with my players and team. Thank You Rob Polishook."

- Bert Strane, former MLB player

"*Baseball Inside The Zone* is a must read for any baseball player looking to perform at their very best. Not only is it a must read, the 33 mental training workouts should be a part of the serious players daily training program. Any practice or workout which doesn't address the mental component of baseball simply falls short in providing the competitive edge needed for success. I've had the privilege of personally working with Rob over the years and have found his methods always highly effective."

- Bob Pigozzi, Owner Pine Brook Baseball and Softball Training Academy

"I worked with Rob during the winter of my senior season, into the early part of spring. I can honestly say that the work I did with him saved my baseball career. He worked closely with me just about every week and really came to understand my struggles and me as a person, not just a client. During my senior season, I broke the school record for saves in a season and ended up making 3rd team all conference. Rob helped me to overcome my mental struggles and helped get me back on track with my pitching performance."

- High School Baseball Player

"Working with you was a great experience that I will always remember. Dealing with the "YIPS" was one of the hardest things I have had to work with in my life. Yet interestingly, I do not regret having it because dealing with it has made me a stronger person, thanks to you."

- College baseball Player

"The only thing that ever held me back throughout my baseball career was my inability to overcome certain mental blocks that most athletes face. It had gotten so bad that I couldn't even play catch without having a million things run through my head. If it wasn't for Rob at Inside the Zone, my career would probably be over. Since I started working with Rob, my performance as well as my confidence has sky rocketed. Thanks to his efforts I can now enjoy playing the game that I have always loved."

- Manny, College baseball player

"The mental game is pivotal to be the best softball player you can be. The weird thing is that the mental game is constantly shoved under the rug yet it's the difference in reaching the next level. Softball and baseball are both games of failure. Getting on base 3 out of 10 times is really good. Yet, that also means you're failing 70% of the time! Elite athletes hate to fail. I know! However, that's why the mental game is so important. It helps you develop the resiliency to ride the highs and lows and reach your goals.

Whenever I felt like I was in a hole, I would refer to the book to bring me back to my feet. The biggest thing was staying present whether it is in class, or on the field. The worksheet in each workout really help to keep you focused on what really matters. Before coming to college, I had never really paid much attention to the mental game. If I would've, I think I could have been that much better. Baseball Inside the Zone will help young softball players (and baseball players) get the edge. "

- D1 College Softball Player

"Two months ago I was thinking about quitting baseball because i was having severe control problems. It was one of the hardest things i had ever experienced. Imagine being a pitcher and spraying the ball all over! Rob helped me remember what it was like to throw like a kid again, loose and relaxed. He reassured me that I wasn't broken but just needed to find my natural rhythm. Through hard work and trusting our process, I am throwing better than ever, in fact last game I was brought in with a runner on third and two out, last inning...I struck him out! I now have more confidence and trust in my ability to bounce back from adversity. i couldnt have done it without Rob, thank you."

- Martin, College baseball pitcher

"What a blessing Rob has been to our family! When my 15 year old son was diagnosed with "Sasser Syndrome", our lives changed forever. As parents our first thought was "what have we done or not done to cause this?" It was heartbreaking to watch my son struggle to throw a baseball 60 feet. He was feeling extremely stressed and even stated that he thought he was going crazy. Out of desperation, I emailed Mackey Sasser for advice. He forwarded my email to Rob Polishook who in return called me and talked at great lengths about Peters situation. When I got off the phone, I was a bit more relieved about the situation but I'll admit I was a bit reluctant to believe that he could help much. However, after working with my son, he is now playing his position as catcher for his high school varsity team and performing very well. As great as this is, the real change I notice in my son is how he now handles stressors and situations that come at him off the field. He no longer sits back and allows unpleasant things to happen to him. He stands up for himself and exhibits increased self esteem. For this, I am forever grateful. In hindsight, I feel this little "monster" appearing out of our life has actually been a blessing in disguise. As hard as it was to experience as a parent, and as a player for my son, the result is a more confident and stronger person. Thank you Rob, for the awesome work you have devoted your life to. I can and will genuinely call you "our miracle worker".

- High School Baseball Mom

" I want to thank you from the bottom of my heart . We thought our sons' college baseball dreams were over, as did he. He was recruited as a left-handed pitcher and was just getting into the beginning of his freshman year when he got the YIPS. In simple terms, a potentially career ending mentally crushing condition that causes a player to basically forget how to throw a ball. After a desperate cry for help we found Rob. Within a very short time, He has Kyle back on track. He has pitched fourteen innings with an era of 1. Thank you so much! Even more amazing, Kyle was undecided on a major and now has decided to go into psychology with a coaching minor. God has a plan and ours was to meet Rob. Thanks again. You helped a really good kid. "

- College Baseball Mom

"As a huge baseball fan and long-time Central Park softball player, I kept thinking while reading Rob Polishook's excellent *Tennis Inside the Zone*, "I wish there was a baseball version of this book." Well, that wish has just been answered! If Yogi Berra was correct in saying that "Ninety percent of the game is half mental," then Polishook's Baseball Inside the Zone is a game-changing resource that will help any softball or baseball player, from Little League to the Major Leagues, to take both their mental game and their on-field performance to the next level. Play ball!"

- Todd Cherches, CEO of BigBlueGumball and Adjunct Professor of leadership a NYU and Columbia University

Biography of the Author

Rob Polishook, M.A., C.P.C., is founder and director of Inside the Zone Sports Performance Group, LLC. As a mental training coach, he works with athletes and teams from junior players to professionals, helping them to uncover their mental edge—often the difference between winning and losing. He specializes in helping athletes overcome performance blocks (i.e. yips, chokes, slumps, anxiety), helping athletes work through the "unspoken" psychological trauma from injuries, helping already high-performing athletes reach beyond self-imposed barriers, and teaching innovative mental training skills, tools, and techniques.

Rob's non-judgmental manner encourages athletes to work with performance issues using awareness, acceptance, and brain/body intuition. This unique inside-out approach encourages empowerment and trust in self and the process. Rob's focus is on the athlete as a person first and a performer second a philosophy he has coined: More than an athlete. Through this lens, he recognizes that day-to-day, on- and off-the-court/field experiences directly impact how an athlete performs, especially under pressure.

Rob works with baseball and softball players of all ages and all levels. His work with former MLB player Mackey Sasser was especially exciting for him. Subsequently, Alex Gibney produced a 30 for 30 ESPN documentary highlighted his and collegues work with Mackey and players with performance blocks, yips and nerves.

Rob first book which was published in 2015 is titled *Tennis Inside the Zone- 32 mental training workouts for Champions*. It is sold internationally. Rob's articles have also been published nationally and internationally and he has been quoted in *Sports Illustrated, NY Times, Newsweek* and other national media. He has also been featured in interviews with ESPN radio and TennisChannel.com.

Rob has earned a Master's degree in psychological studies with a concentration in sport and exercise psychology from Seton Hall University (SHU), and has completed his certification in sport psychology from SHU. He is a certified professional/life coach from IPEC, an international federation coaching affiliate. He has also received certifications in Somatic Experiencing, Brainspotting Sports Performance Work, Focusing and Jim Loehr's Mental Toughness Program, Mindfulness and Animal communication.

Rob and his wife Debbie live in New York City. He can often be spotted in Central Park with his wife Debbie and dog Gumbo.

Rob relaxing with Deb and Gumbo after the release
of Baseball Inside the Zone.

About Inside the Zone Sports Performance Group

Founded in 2005, Inside the Zone Sports Performance Group was born from Rob Polishook's passion for sports, his love of working with kids, and his curiosity in understanding the process of what it takes to help athletes break beyond barriers. The goal of Inside the Zone Sports Performance Group is to assist athletes, in all sports and at all levels, to uncover their mental edge and unleash their unlimited peak performance.

The mental side plays a large role in any sport. In fact, with all the club teams and increased specialization among teams, it is interesting, and even remiss, that the real mental issues regarding competition among young athletes are not being addressed. These issues include, but are not limited to, competing under pressure; handling setbacks and using them to bounce back; concentrating under pressure; staying centered; focusing on the process and not on the scoreboard; crafting strategies for goal setting; and reaching beyond self-imposed barriers toward limitless peak potential. Inside the Zone Sports Performance Group's mission is to address these issues and more.

Inside the Zone Sports Performance Group services:

- One-on-one and group consultations for athletes, parents, and coaches

- Workshops and seminars for teams, parents, and coaches

- Dynamic season-long consultations for teams

Rob Polishook, M.A., C.P.C.
Mental Training Coach
www.insidethezone.com
rob@insidethezone.com

Instagram/Twitter: @insidethezone,
Facebook: Inside the zone

Bring it!

Bring More

Bring Your More

More than an Athlete

About Rob: The Back Story

Who am I?

I was born imperfect—or maybe perfectly imperfect! Here's a great example from my first grade class trip: All I remember is spinning around a revolving door at the Empire State Building, getting my shoe caught and holding up everyone from access to the door for three minutes, while being laughed at by my class. Then, back in the classroom, I was unable to read: the letters were a jumbled mess, teachers would get frustrated, and I was ashamed to raise my hand. I was diagnosed with a form of dyslexia and a motor learning problem.

I vividly remember being left behind in first grade, and attempting to explain the reason to my friends. Even clearer was my memory of getting special tutoring from Mrs. Schaffer after school on reading, writing and arithmetic. Going into third grade I couldn't read or write cursive, and this presented a problem. It felt like I was in a foreign country. The only place I might have felt normal was Hebrew school, but here I didn't understand the letters either! In my spare time, I remember balancing on a board, the kind with a roller underneath, which was supposed to help with my coordination and balance.

I did these types of exercises my entire childhood! Extra work was something that was part of my upbringing. I never had time to feel sorry for myself or ask why I was different; I just went to the extra tutoring and got on my balance board for hours.

I learned at an early age never, never, never to give up. I never let an opportunity for extra credit pass by. And I never stopped training at anything I cared about.

I was lucky. At an early age I experienced what it was like to have a strong support system, with parents who believed in me. Because of my learning disabilities, I learned to be empathetic to others who didn't get things done as fast or as well as the rest of the class.

Why am I writing this book?

Every day, I hear athletes tell me about their fears, anxieties, and performance blocks. I hear how they stand on a pitcher's mound feeling like they are on a deserted island; or how they constantly get caught in a negative spiral during pressure situations. It reminds me of how when I was a kid, I wished I had someone I could open up to and let them know how I was feeling and experience a situation from my point of view. Instead, my coaches always told me how I was supposed to be feeling and what I could or couldn't do. If nothing else, a book like this would have been valuable just to have an outlet to let go, and in some cases verify what I was thinking was "normal."

After I listen to what my clients are saying, I usually express to them that they are not alone in what they are thinking and feeling; in fact, it's often shared by many athletes in the same situation on all levels. This reassurance usually makes them feel like a 500-pound weight has been lifted off their shoulders.

Acknowledgements

A book like this doesn't happen without the support and encouragement from many people. First, and foremost I'd like to thank Ryan Sliwak, whom I initially met as a student in my graduate class at Seton Hall University. Years later, Ryan approached me to adapt Tennis Inside the Zone to Baseball Inside the Zone. Simply put, this book doesn't happen without Ryan driving it. His enthusiasm, expertise, drive, and focus on the mental side of baseball and psychology is what brought this book to the finish line. Ryan was instrumental in its development including research, quotes, and anything baseball. He knows the game like no other and aspires to bring awareness to the myriad of mental health issues that young athletes confront. This leads to Matt Rothenburg, former Harvard baseball player who contributed key ideas, developmental thoughts, and edits all during his senior year at school and while playing on the team. Matt was like the middle reliever, he has a bright future ahead of him. Special thanks to Ivana Vinnick, another student of mine at Seton Hall. Her steadfast ideas, attention to detail, and edits kept Baseball Inside the Zone consistent and on a schedule throughout the process. Ivana was like a short reliever. She also has a great future in the field of performance psychology.

Big thanks to Kellie Patterson, she has been instrumental in all graphic development and idea generation of both Tennis and now Baseball Inside the Zone. Her "can-do" attitude, enthusiasm, and joy to continually contribute ideas to Inside the Zone is greatly appreciated.

Thanks to Dr. Alan Goldberg a great mentor and long-time friend always encouraging and teaching me, especially the foundational idea that an athlete is a person first and a performer second! Thank you, David Grande, developer of Brain-spotting. Special thanks to John Martini who is always available to share ideas, trends, and critique my work. Thanks to Dr. Sandra Lee, Dr. Riley Nickols, and Dr. Jerry Lynch who has always been supportive, and encouraging of my work.

Thanks to Mackey Sasser and every one of my clients in all sports. Mackey has been a great friend over the years since David, Alan, and myself worked together, and Alex Gibney produced Fields of Fear for ESPN's 30 for 30 series.

Thanks to my Dad, Shim-shon, and my Mum, Jean: her devotion to inspire others lives inside of me. My brother Mark, sister Janis, sister/brother-in-laws Sandy, Lenny, and our precious nieces and nephews.

Big hug and thanks to my bride of 33 years, Debbie. None of this work could ever have begun without your unconditional love, support, and belief in me. You listen to all my crazy ideas and encourage me to pursue most of them! You have been my rock of stability. Lastly, thanks to Gumbo, she patiently sits in my office as I work with clients, and write.

When you bring who you are to
what you do, more happens!

Sources

Below is a listing of books which have influenced me and inspired *Baseball Inside the Zone*. All quotes have sources attached, if by chance something was omitted, please note it was not on purpose and we will correct in future printings.

- Andracki, T. (2015, September 05). Cubs Think Arrieta Can Get Even Better. Retrieved from https://www.nbcsports.com/chicago/chicago-cubs/cubs-think-jake-arrieta-can-actually-get-even-better.

- Ankiel, Rick. (2017, September 28). Letter to My Younger Self. Retrieved from https://www.theplayerstribune.com/en-us/articles/rick-ankiel-letter-to-my-younger-self-cardinals.

- Associated Press. (2017, October 11). Jose Altuve Staying Humble As Astros Marvel At 2b Ahead of ALCS. Retrieved from http://www.espn.com/mlb/story/_/id/20993726/2017-mlb-postseason-jose-altuve-staying-moment-houston-astros-marvel-2b.

- Baseball Almanac: The History of Major League Baseball (n.d.). Retrieved from http://www.baseball-almanac.com

- Baumann, M. (2017, October 29). Wood, Morton, and Giles All Surprise in Game 4-for Better or for Worse. Retrieved from https://www.theringer.com/mlb/2017/10/29/16566024/wood-morton-and-giles-all-surprise-in-game-4-for-better-or-for-worse.

- Berra, Y., Kaplan, D. (2003). What Time is it? You Mean Now?: Advice for Life from the Zen Master of Them All. Rockefeller Center, NY: Simon & Schuster.

- Bowman, M. (2017, August 16). Staying Positive, Swanson Collects Pair of Hits. Retrieved from https://www.mlb.com/news/braves-dansby-swanson-staying-positive/c-248726090.

- Cain, B., Byrnes, E. (2017, January 17). Eric Byrnes – A Major League Endurance Sports Mindset. @Brian Cain's Peak Performance Podcast. Podcast retrieved from https://briancain.com/blog/bc-115-eric-byrnes-a-major-league-mindset.html

- Cain, B., Corbin, T. (n.d.). Tim Corbin on Coaching the Mental Game. @ Brian Cain's Peak Performance Podcast. Podcast retrieved from https://briancain.com/blog/bc118-tim-corbin-on-coaching-the-mental-game.html

- Cain, B., Ravizza, K. (n.d.). Ken Ravizza- Heads up Baseball. @ Brian Cain's Peak Performance Podcast. Podcast retrieved from https://briancain.com/blog/bc146-ken-ravizza-heads-up-baseball-2-0.html.

- Canfield, J. Hansen, M. Donnelly, M. (2012). Chicken Soup for the Baseball Fan's Soul: Inspirational Stories of Baseball, Big- League Dreams and the Game of Life (Chicken Soup for the Soul). Deerfield Beach, FL: Health Communications Inc.

- Caple, J. (2014, September 11). Batting Practice: Swings and Misses. Retrieved from http://www.espn.com/mlb/story/_/id/11503846/mlb-batting-practice-game-game.

- Castillo, J. (2017, June 1). Daniel Murphy and His Never-Ending Pursuit of the Perfect Swing. The Washington Post. Retrieved from https://www.washingtonpost.com/news/nationals-journal/wp/2017/06/01/daniel-murphy-and-his-never-ending-pursuit-of-the-perfect-swing/?utm_term=.d1a2bc131bf6.

- Causi, A. (2017, December 7). Aaron Boone Introduced: Yankees Skipper Embraces High Expectations. The New York Post. Retrieved from https://nypost.com/2017/12/06/aaaron-boone-introduced-as-yankees-manager-how-well-take-next-step/.

- Cohen, P. (2013, October 14). Resiliency: Bouncing Back from a Bad Game. Retrieved from http://www.baseballmentalgame.com/featured-mental-game-articles/resiliency-bouncing-back-from-a-bad-game/.

- Cohen, P (2016, October 11). The Mental Skill of Focusing. Retrieved from http://www.baseballmentalgame.com/featured-mental-game-articles/texas-rangers-win-today-focus/.

- Cornetta, L. (2011, September 6). C.J Wilson Routine, In His Words. Retrieved from http://www.espn.com/dallas/mlb/story/_/id/6934822/texas-rangers-cj-wilson-explains-routine-detail.

- Cut4 Staff. (2017, April 20). Rick Ankiel Talks the Yips, Anxiety and What it was like to Start Over. Retreived from https://www.mlb.com/cut4/rick-ankiel-book-the-phenomenon-interview/c-225450894.

- Davadi, D. (n.d.). Body by Bautista. Retrieved from https://www.sportsnet.ca/baseball/mlb/jose-bautista-dominates-body-maintenance-game/.

- Edwards Jr., E. (2017, February 21). Why I Fly the W So Hard. The Players Tribune. Retrieved from https://www.theplayerstribune.com/en-us/articles/carl-edwards-jr-cubs-fly-the-w.

- Fleming, D. (2017, March 1). Tim Tebow's Relentless Pursuit of Failure. Retrieved from http://www.espn.com/mlb/story/_/id/18791367/tim-tebow-relentless-pursuit-failure

- Fletcher, J. (2017, April 9). Angels Use Seven-Run Ninth Inning to Stun Mariners, 10-9. Orange County Register. Retrieved from https://www.ocregister.com/2017/04/09/angels-rally-for-7-in-the-bottom-of-the-9th-to-stun-mariners/.

- Fox Sports. (2018, February 26). Astros Lefty Keuchel Constantly Studying and Learning. Retrieved from https://www.foxsports.com/mlb/story/astros-lefty-keuchel-constantly-studying-and-learning-022618.

- Fox Sports. (2014, June 17). Do We Give Momentum Too Much Credit in Baseball? Retrieved from https://www.foxsports.com/mlb/story/do-we-give-momentum-too-much-credit-in-baseball-061714.

- Gonzales, M. Sullivan, P. (2015, September 26). Say it Again, Joe: 11 of Our Favorite Maddonisms. The Chicago Tribune. Retrieved from http://www.chicagotribune.com/sports/baseball/cubs/ct-cubs-maddonisms-spt-0927-20150924-story.html.

- Grialou, C. (2017, November 7). New Manager Torey Lovullo Sees 'Special Talent' on Arizona Diamondbacks. Retrieved from http://arizonasports.com/story/891775/torey-lovullo-sees-special-talent-arizona-diamondbacks/.

- Hall, B. (2017, February 01). Cleveland Indians Closer Cody Allen Reveals His Secret to Handling Pressure. Retrieved from http://www.stack.com/a/cleveland-indians-closer-cody-allen-reveals-his-secret-to-handling-pressure.

- Hanson, T., Ravizza, K. (1998). Heads-up Baseball: Playing the Game One Pitch at a Time. Chicago, IL: Masters Press.

- Harrell, I. (2009, June 24). Joey Votto Makes His Personal Demons Public. Retrieved from https://bleacherreport.com/articles/205520-joey-votto-makes-his-personal-demons-public.

- Hart, T. (2018, March 15). Hart: The True Essence of Augie Garrdio. Retrieved from https://d1baseball.com/columns/hart-true-essence-augie-garrido/.

- Haudricourt, T. (2016, October 4). Brewers Defined Success Differently in 2016. Milwaukee Journal Sentinel. Retrieved from https://www.jsonline.com/story/sports/mlb/brewers/2016/10/04/brewers-defined-success-differently-2016/91485372/.

- Justice, Richard. (2001 April 22). Knoblauch, Ankiel not First Players to Lose it. The Houston Chronicle. Retrieved from https://www.chron.com/news/article/Knoblauch-Ankiel-not-first-players-to-lose-it-2052986.php.

- Kelly, C. (2007, March 12). Halladay: A Master of Detail. Retrieved from https://www.thestar.com/sports/2007/03/12/halladay_a_master_of_detail.html.

- Keri, J. (2017, February 9). Q&A with Rajai Davis: Rickey Henderson, the Art of Base Stealing and Getting to MLB. Retrieved from https://www.cbssports.com/mlb/news/q-a-with-rajai-davis-rickey-henderson-the-art-of-base-stealing-and-getting-to-mlb/.

- Kerr-Dineen, L. (2016, February 9). The 48 Greatest Quotes About Winning. USA Today. Retrieved from https://ftw.usatoday.com/2016/02/best-sports-quotes-about-winning.

- Kuenster, R. (2015). Baseball's Top 10: Ranking the Best Major League Player by Position. Lanham, MD: The Rowman and Littlefield Publishing Group.

- Kurkjian, T. (2013, May 2). Baseball's Symphony of Sounds. Retrieved from http://www.espn.com/mlb/story/_/id/9190902/sounds-major-league-baseball-game-players-perspective.

- Levine, B. (2018, May 12). White Sox Aim to Not Let Losing Spiral Inhibit Player Development. Retrieved from https://670thescore.radio.com/articles/white-sox-aim-not-let-losing-spiral-inhibit-player-development.

- Pavlovic, A. (2017, March). Rollins Sharp in Spring Debut at Second Base; 'Let the Instincts Take Over'. Retrieved from https://www.nbcsports.com/bayarea/giants/rollins-sharp-spring-debut-second-base-let-instincts-take-over.

- Perry, D. (2017, October 29). Yankee Legend Mariano Rivera Talks Cutter, Playoff Pressure, mound Visits and More. Retrieved from https://www.cbssports.com/mlb/news/yankees-legend-mariano-rivera-talks-cutter-playoff-pressure-mound-visits-and-more/.

- Marchand, A. (2017, 18 July). Inside Dirt: Aaron Judge Has A Secret Plan to Break His Slump. Retrieved from http://www.espn.com/mlb/story/_/id/20091290/here-dirt-new-york-yankees-aaron-judge.

- Mayo, J. (2014, April 28). Springer Brings Perspective to Life and Baseball. Retrieved from https://www.mlb.com/news/astros-outfielder-george-springer-overcame-stutter/c-73428538.

- McCaffery, Jen. (2015, May 18). Boston Red Sox Make Players' Mental Health A Focal Point this Season. Retrieved from http://www.masslive.com/redsox/index.ssf/2015/05/boston_red_sox_mental_health.html.

- Mccullough, A. (2017, January 27). Rich Hill's Baseball Resurrection. The Pitcher's Odyssey from Failure to a $48 Million Dodgers Contract. LA Times. Retrieved from http://www.latimes.com/sports/dodgers/la-sp-dodgers-rich-hill-profile-20170127-htmlstory.html.

- McMananman, B. (2018, April 23). Diamondbacks Relying on David Peraltas's Energy, Positive Mindset During Red-Hot Start. Retrieved from https://www.azcentral.com/story/sports/mlb/diamondbacks/2018/04/23/arizona-diamondbacks-david-peralta-torey-lovullo/542859002/.

- Mears, G. (2015, November 20). Bryce Harper: "If They're Not Laughing at Your Dreams, You're Not Dreaming Big Enough". Retrieved from http://www.talknats. com/2015/11/20/bryce-harper-if-theyre-not-laughing-at-your-dreams-youre-not-dreaming-big-enough/.

- Miller, B. (2017, February 24). The Neuroscience Behind Cubs' Mindfulness and Mental Skills Initiatives. Retrieved from https://www.cubsinsider.com/2017/02/24/ neuroscience-behind-cubs-mindfulness-mental-skills-initiatives/.

- Miller, Scott. (2015, May 11). The Mental ABCs of Postmodern Baseball: Searching for Every Possible Edge. Retrieved from http://bleacherreport.com/articles/2458725-the-mental-abcs-of-postmodern-baseball-searching-for-every-possible-edge.

- Mitrolis, T. (2009, August 6). Mental Mastery: Even Longoria's Leap to Stardom. Retrieved from https://bleacherreport.com/articles/231526-mental-mastery-evan-longorias-leap-to-stardom.

- MLB Network. (2017, May 26). Josh Donaldson Discusses the Evolution of His Swing (Video file). Retrieved from https://www.youtube.com/watch?v=iFllxmlUq08.

- MLB Network. (2016, October 11). MLB Tonight: Panic on Comeback Win (video file). Retrieved from https://www.facebook.com/MLBNetwork/ videos/10153764572481695/.

- Moeller, C. (2013, August 20). Control What You Can Control. Retrieved from http:// www.chadmoellerbaseball.com/instructional-baseball-blog/control-what-you-can-control/.

- Montemurro, M. (2015, June 4). What Drives Joathan Papelbon? 'Fear of Failure'. USA Today. Retrieved from https://www.usatoday.com/story/sports/mlb/2015/06/04/ jonathan-papelbon-full--confidence/28479655/.

- Moreno, M. (2014, October, 2014). Corey Seager Learned from Failure to Find Success. Retrieved from http://www.dodgersnation.com/corey-seager-learned-from-failure-to-find-success/2014/10/25/.

- Norris, D. (2016, April 7). More Than Just the 'Man in the Van'. The Players Tribune. Retrieved from https://www.theplayerstribune.com/en-us/articles/daniel-norris-tigers-pitcher-baseball-van.

- Olney, B. (2014, March 20). Creative Control. Retrieved from http://www.espn.com/ espn/feature/story/_/id/10619342/creative-control-clayton-kershaw-abides-strict-code.

- Ortiz, Jorge L. (2015, July 5). Robinson Cano's Trying Year: Lingering Illness, Grandfather's Death Test Him. USA Today. Retrieved from https://www.usatoday.com/story/sports/mlb/2015/07/05/robinson-cano-acid-reflux-struggle-grandfather/29745307/.

- Oz, M. (2017, July 14). Didi Gregorius on Aaron Judge, his Keys to Success and Life in New York. @ StewPod Baseball Podcast. Podcast retrieved from https://sports.yahoo.com/podcast-didi-gregorius-aaron-judge-keys-success-life-new-york-222752780.html.

- Oz, M (2017, October 26). How Justin Verlander, George Springer, and A Little Faith May Have Saved the Astros' Season. Retrieved from https://sports.yahoo.com/justin-verlander-george-springer-little-faith-may-saved-astros-season-080711624.html.

- Pavlovic, A. (2017, March 2). Rollins Sharp in Spring Debut at Second Base: 'Let the Instincts Take Over'. Retrieved from https://www.nbcsports.com/bayarea/giants/rollins-sharp-spring-debut-second-base-let-instincts-take-over.

- Ravizza, K. (2018, February 27). 15 Critical Questions on the Mental Game of Baseball (Video file). Retrieved from https://www.youtube.com/watch?v=cYFw9bHtNlw

- Ross, D., Yager, D., (2017) Teammates: My Journey in Baseball and a World Series. New York, NY: Hachette Book Group.

- Rivera, J. (2017, October 18). MLB Playoffs: Yankees, One Win from World Series, Hope to Break ALCS Trend in Houston. Retrieved from http://www.sportingnews.com/mlb/news/yankees-astros-game-5-6-alcs-todd-frazier-houston-momentum-aaron-judge/for6hdlcylee1nuccxybgrzmq.

- Robinson, Tom. (2016, February 15). Solving the Mental Game in an At-Bat. Retrieved from http://theseason.gc.com/baseball-solving-the-mental-game-in-an-at-bat.

- Salisbury, J. (2018, April 3). Gabe Kapler Appears Humbled, Calls First Series a Learning Experience. Retrieved from https://sports.yahoo.com/gabe-kapler-appears-humbled-calls-235011205.html.

- SB Nation. (2013, January 30th). Interview with Atlanta Braves Closer Craig Kimbrel: Part 2. Retrieved from https://www.talkingchop.com/2013/1/30/3930798/interview-with-atlanta-braves-closer-craig-kimbrel-part-2.

- Schoenfeld, B. (2017, September 28). Here Comes the Closer…In the Seventh Inning? The New York Times. Retrieved from https://www.nytimes.com/2017/09/28/magazine/here-comes-the-closer-in-the-seventh-inning.html.

- Serby, S. (2015, October 2). Michael Conforto on Life as a Rookie, NAVY Seal Breathing Exercises, and Russel Wilson. The New York Post. Retrieved from https://nypost.com/2015/10/04/michael-conforto-on-life-as-a-rookie-navy-seal-breathing-exercises-and-russell-wilson/.

- Shepatin, M (2015, May). Know the Power of Mental Imagery. Retrieved from http://bigthink.com/the-wheelhouse/3-important-life-lessons-learned-in-my-13-years-as-a-major-league-pitcher.

- Smoltz, J., Yaeger, D. (2013). Starting and Closing: Perseverance, Faith, and One More Year. New York, NY: HarperCollins Publishers.

- Steward, C. (2014, August 21). A's Lefty Jon Lester, Formerly with Red Sox, Knows All About Hype. The Mercury News. Retrieved from https://www.mercurynews.com/2014/08/21/as-lefty-jon-lester-formerly-with-red-sox-knows-all-about-hype/.

- Street, H. (2005, June 2). Handling the 'Pressure" of the Ninth Inning. Retrieved from http://www.espn.com/mlb/columns/story?columnist=street_huston&id=2073394.

- Sullivan, P. (2017, February 12). MLB 2017 storylines: Cubs Have Target on Their Backs as They Attempt to Repeat. The Chicago Tribune. Retrieved from http://www.chicagotribune.com/sports/columnists/ct-mlb-storylines-cubs-repeat-sullivan-spt-0212-20170211-column.html.

- Talking Hitting with Stan Musial and Tony Gwynn. (2009, July 11). Sporting News. Retrieved from http://www.sportingnews.com/mlb/news/108638-talking-hitting-stan-musial-and-tony-gwynn.

- Umoh, R. (2017, November 2). The Uplifting Message the Dodgers Manager Gave his Team After Losing the World Series. Retrieved from https://www.cnbc.com/2017/11/02/what-the-dodgers-manager-told-his-team-after-losing-the-world-series.html.

- WFAA Staff. (2017, May 31). So, I talked to Jeff Banister About Bullpen Usage. It's May 31st Baseball Texas Daily. WFAA ABC8. Retrieved from https://www.wfaa.com/article/sports/mlb/rangers/so-i-talked-to-jeff-banister-about-bullpen-usage-its-the-may-31st-baseball-texas-daily/444626598.

- Wyllys, J. (2018, April 30). Going Mental: How MLB Players Have Embraced Psychology to Mange High Stress. Retrieved from http://www.sportingnews.com/mlb/news/mlb-mental-skills-coaches-psychologists-methods-white-sox-jeffrey-fishbein-ben-zobrist/1jb1by8kumjhe10r4ncb90bn49.

- Yang, N. (2017, October 8). Kevin Millar Talks Playoff Baseball, Shares his Advice for this Year's Sox, and Sheds Light on his Current Endeavors. Retrieved from https://www.boston.com/sports/boston-red-sox/2017/10/08/kevin-millars-advice-for-the-red-sox-is-to-block-out-the-noise.

- Zwelling, A. (2016, 14, October). Donaldson's Instinct, Experience Making a Difference in Blue Jays' Post-Season. Retrieved from https://www.sportsnet.ca/baseball/mlb/donaldsons-instinct-experience-making-difference-blue-jays-post-season/.